8/93

WITHDRAWN

 St. Louis Community College

Forest Park
Florissant Valley
Meramec

Instructional Resources
St. Louis, Missouri

Born a Chief

Edmund Nequatewa

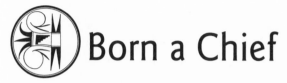 # Born a Chief

THE NINETEENTH CENTURY
HOPI BOYHOOD OF
EDMUND NEQUATEWA

As Told to Alfred F. Whiting
Edited by P. David Seaman

The University of Arizona Press

Tucson & London

Frontispiece: Edmund Nequatewa in 1934. (Courtesy of the
Museum of Northern Arizona, photo no. 9501)

The University of Arizona Press
Copyright © 1993
The Arizona Board of Regents

⊗ This book is printed on acid-free, archival-quality paper.
Manufactured in the United States of America

98 97 96 95 94 93   6 5 4 3 2 1

Library of Congress Cataloging-in-Publication Data
Nequatewa, Edmund, ca. 1880–1969.
    Born a chief : the nineteenth century Hopi boyhood of Edmund
Nequatewa, as told to Alfred F. Whiting / edited by P. David Seaman.
       p. cm.
    Includes bibliographical references (p.   ) and index.
    ISBN 0-8165-1327-9 (Cl : acid-free, archival-quality paper). —
    ISBN 0-8165-1354-6 (Pbk : acid-free, archival-quality paper)
       1. Nequatewa Edmund, ca. 1880–1969. 2. Hopi Indians—Biography.
    I. Whiting, Alfred F.   II. Seaman, P. David.   III. Title.
    E99.H7N45   1993   92-25863
    978.9'004974—dc20   CIP

British Cataloguing-in-Publication Data
A catalogue record for this book is available from the British Library.

For my esteemed sister,
Dr. Ruth Anne Seaman Smith

Contents

REFERENCE MATERIALS

Figures

Foreword

Autobiographical accounts are known to us from records extending well over four thousand years. These include Egyptian life stories on the walls of tombs, Hittite and Assyrian royal accounts on clay tablets, and of course Julius Caesar's account of his conquest of Gaul. Through the centuries, scholars and lay readers alike have found these autobiographies very valuable. The history that they contain is biased, to be sure, but we relate more closely to someone who is telling about something that he himself or she herself actually did.

The account presented here is an unusual one, as it is by a Hopi, whose people have not historically had a tradition of literacy. The Hopi are, of course, literate due to their exposure to English, but the preservation of the spoken word in Hopi is limited. The potential is there, but whether a wider Hopi literature is created is entirely up to the people themselves. For it to happen, the Hopi must find it to be of value for their own culture.

The present volume, being in English, cannot be considered true Hopi literature. Actually, it is an example of oral literature, having been dictated to a scholar, who then wrote it down. It is important to note that implicit in the narrator's willingness to do this is his wish to pass on his experiences, both to his own people and to others.

This book is therefore a record of spoken language, but it is also a voice from a past generation, and in this lies its primary value. Just as the Hopi once adapted to life in the high-desert area in which they now live, today they are adapting to the wide range of cultural values that surround them.

Change is part of human culture, and one cannot deny its force. Those involved in the process will inevitably lose many features of the older culture. I hope the account given here will provide an opportunity for members of the younger generation of Hopi to "listen" to someone whom they have never known, to an elder telling them of his experiences. The Hopi have demonstrated an admirable adherence to many beliefs and practices fundamental to their special character as a people. Perhaps the younger Hopi who read this narrative will find that doing so increases their interest in these traditional values.

Though this account is sure to be of considerable importance to the Hopi, it will inevitably also be of interest to a much wider audience. European (and derivative American) culture is omnivorous: things are read for the sake of learning, whatever it is that may be learned. Nothing human is considered alien, and this account is an intensely human story.

I emphasize that this story recalls only one man's experiences. It is not meant to offer a philosophy or a worldview. It is a personal narrative, here presented as a contribution to the growing list of more permanent records of earlier Hopi life and culture. It is not ancient history or ancient legend but a reflection of the near past, which has been preserved by a dedicated scholar who had a deep appreciation of the Hopi way of life. We are greatly indebted to the Hopi elder who shared his experiences with us in this account, and to Alfred Whiting, who recorded it.

CARLETON T. HODGE
Indiana University

Acknowledgments

Many individuals and institutions have aided in the preparation of this book over the past fifty years. Alfred Whiting was always generous with his praise of patient librarians and his many friends and acquaintances who helped in various ways with his research. Many of these have already been thanked publicly in the acknowledgments to his book *Havasupai Habitat,* edited by Steven A. Weber and P. David Seaman and published in 1985.

In Whiting's notes and later versions of his manuscript of *Born a Chief,* he expressed appreciation for the assistance of Sterling MacIntosh, a student from Prescott who helped with the initial recordings, and for the later help of Mary E. Wesbrook and Mildred Bueddeman of Dartmouth College, Katharine Bartlett and Dorothy House of the Museum of Northern Arizona Library, Robert C. Euler, and Barton A. Wright.

The present version of this book was made possible through considerable financial support from Northern Arizona University and the consistent encouragement of many individuals there, including President Eugene Hughes, Vice Presidents Patsy Reed and Henry Hooper, Director of University Libraries Jean Collins, Dean Earl Backman of the College of Social and Behavioral Sciences,

Anthropology Department Chair Robert Trotter II, Professors Reed Riner of the Anthropology Department and Stanley Swarts of the Geography Department, and Joan Gorman of the Northern Arizona University Foundation.

Advice and encouragement were also received from James Glenn and Ives Goddard, both of the Smithsonian Institution in Washington, D.C.

As editor of the final version, I received excellent advice and suggestions from Carleton and Pat Hodge at Indiana University, William and Helen Hodge in Flagstaff, Gail Rusnak and Sharon Lindsey in the Department of Anthropology at Northern Arizona University, and my research assistant, Alyssa Byrkit, as well as from the excellent editorial staff at the University of Arizona Press. One other person read the manuscript again and again, double-checked references, made photocopies endlessly, and provided timely food and moral support; without the intelligent and loving assistance of my wife Mary Miller Seaman the book simply would not have been finished.

Al Whiting touched many lives in many positive ways. His bequest to me of his incredibly extensive ethnographic fieldwork notes and papers changed the recent course of my career. The fifteen-year task of compiling and editing is now drawing to a close, and an agreement has been signed to house the entire Whiting Collection in the Special Collections and Archives Department of the Cline Library at Northern Arizona University for the benefit of other researchers interested in the Hopi people.

The many Hopis who helped with this project will out of courtesy remain anonymous. But in their honor, no attempt will be made to recover research costs. All royalties beyond actual publication and sales costs have been irrevocably assigned to an endowed scholarship fund for Hopi students at Northern Arizona University.

P. DAVID SEAMAN
Northern Arizona University

Introduction

This is the true story of the boyhood of a Hopi Indian during the latter part of the nineteenth century. Edmund Nequatewa was born around 1880 in a remote Second Mesa village on the Hopi reservation in northern Arizona. For the historical reasons recounted in Chapter 2, Edmund was automatically in line to be chief of a Hopi society. This brought added responsibility to the young boy, but also family and community jealousy and various attempts either to aid or thwart his destiny.

This book gives Edmund's account of his tumultuous life from his birth to about age twenty-two, shortly after he had returned home from a forced education at the Phoenix Indian School. It richly portrays the experiences of a Hopi boy caught up in early conflicts involving his family, the Hopi people, and a rapidly changing world. The reader will gain insights into early Hopi life and the personal and community changes brought about by agents of the United States Government, especially in regard to early Indian health, education, and welfare.

The Hopi Indians have lived in northeastern Arizona for more than a thousand years. Today, more than 7,000 tribal members occupy a dozen pueblo-type villages, most of which are located on high mesas along an eighty-mile stretch of Arizona State Highway 264 between Keams Canyon on the east and Tuba City on the west (see map).[1]

The origin of the Hopi people is shrouded in myth and mystery. One frequent account has them emerging from another world through a hole in the floor of the Grand Canyon; another account has some of them arriving by boat from southern ports of origin across the Gulf of Mexico.[2] The evidence from linguistics and from the Hopi's own folk literature indicates that the Hopi are an amalgam of related groups who arrived in what is now Arizona more than a thousand years ago from several different directions.

The Hopi are members of the large Uto-Aztecan language group. Their relatives include the Utes to the north, the Pima and Tohono O'odham to the south, and the Aztec groups far to the south.

Beginning in the late 1500s, the Spanish sought to missionize and colonize the pueblo tribes in New Mexico. These efforts met with only limited success and engendered among the pueblo groups a great deal of hostility toward them. Finally, in 1680 the New Mexico pueblos—joined by the Arizona Hopi—revolted and drove the Spanish from their territory. Missionary priests who did not manage to escape were killed.

After this, the Hopi lived in fear of reprisals by the Spanish and moved their villages from the foot of the mesas to their top, where they could better protect themselves. As a further effort to preserve their religious and cultural traditions, each main Hopi village established nearby satellite villages with which they were interdependent but which had their own political chiefs and religious priests, who

1. Part of this brief description is taken from "Hopi Background Sketch" in my *Hopi dictionary* (1985).
2. Some Hopi believe that in the underworld from which they came the seasons are reversed from what they are in this world. This may be further evidence that some Hopi ancestors originally lived south of the equator.

were responsible for preserving all aspects of the Hopi way of life. In spite of these defensive measures, the Spanish slaughtered selected Hopi men from Shungopovi in reprisal for the Hopi participation in the revolt. Edmund recounts this slaughter in Chapter 2, and in fact it helped set the stage for his birthright as a chief.

Later, increasing Anglo contacts with the western Indians during the early 1800s forced the fledgling United States government to seek solutions to the thorny "Indian question" in the midst of severely conflicting principles and philosophies.[3] In an ongoing national debate, some leaders advocated total assimilation with the "civilized" white man; others advocated total separation and removal of all eastern Indians to territory west of the Mississippi— land already occupied by other tribes. Problems worsened as a result of efforts of politicized church missionary boards. After much deliberation and indecision, a reservation system finally evolved as the most practical solution from the white man's point of view.

The original Hopi reservation was established by executive order in 1882, at about the time of Edmund Nequatewa's birth. Political squabbling between representatives of the Presbyterian and Mormon churches, and other Anglo vested interests, caused the federal government considerable delay in establishing a strong influence among the Hopi. Edmund's account of his childhood during this period gives several glimpses into the government's gradually increasing control of Hopi reservation affairs involving health and other matters, especially education.

For various reasons, both sincere and selfish, the federal government and religious missionaries believed they had an urgent obliga-

---

3. Many books and articles have been written on this subject. For a general overview of federal Indian policy before the Civil War, see Robert Trennert's *Alternative to extinction* (1975). For the years after the Civil War, see Francis P. Prucha's *American Indian policy in crisis* (1976). For late-nineteenth-century developments directly affecting the Hopi, see Stephen McCluskey's 1980 article in the *Journal of Arizona History*.

tion to educate the "savage" Indian children. Their primary goal was to help the children assimilate into the white man's culture and thus receive all its supposed benefits. In the late nineteenth century the federal government, along with several religious groups, began supporting schools for Indian students, some in or near the reservations and some quite far away.

On the Hopi reservation, parents often resisted these educational overtures by secreting their children in closets or other hiding places in their homes. Nevertheless, government agents forcibly removed many Hopi children to nearby day schools or boarding schools and also exerted pressure to have Hopi children sent to places such as Albuquerque for their schooling.

Edmund Nequatewa, urged on by his grandfather, who had been made a member of the school board, was among the first students to attend the new Hopi school at Keams Canyon. Later he attended the Phoenix Indian School, which had opened in 1891.[4] Edmund's accounts of these early programs for Indian education provide rich insights into the attitudes of the typical white educator of that period.

Although the Hopi were originally assigned over 2,500,000 acres for their reservation, their allotted land was completely surrounded by the Navajo reservation. After extensive encroachment by the much larger Navajo group, the Hopi are currently living on only about 500,000 acres. A series of lawsuits between the two tribes over landholding is yet to be settled. The "joint-use" area established by the federal courts in 1963 is now occupied mainly by the Navajo.

Reference to the Hopi villages along Arizona State Highway 264 is usually made according to the mesa on which they are located, starting from the east at Keams Canyon. Keams Canyon contains

4. See Robert Trennert's *The Phoenix Indian School* (1988).

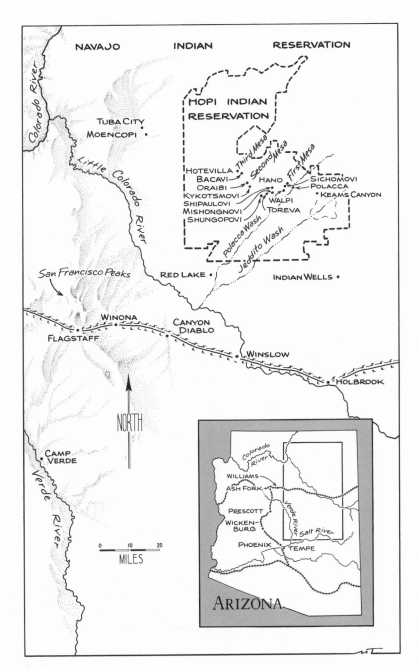

The Hopi reservation and Arizona (Map by Michael Taylor)

the main Hopi offices of the U. S. Bureau of Indian Affairs, as well as a hospital and other federal services. First Mesa includes Hano (a Hopi-Tewa community related to pueblo groups in New Mexico), Sichomovi, Walpi, and Polacca. Second Mesa includes Mishongnovi, Shipaulovi, Shungopovi, the Toreva area, and Second Mesa (which is more modern, being located along the highway). Third Mesa includes Kykotsmovi (New Oraibi, the Hopi tribal headquarters), Old Oraibi (the oldest continuously inhabited town in the United States), Bacavi, Hotevilla, and Moencopi (just south of the Tuba City crossroads at U.S. Route 160).[5]

The environment of all Hopi villages could be classified as high desert. The chief occupations are arts and crafts, sheep and cattle ranching, and gardening. Only around the westernmost village of Moencopi is irrigation prevalent.

Although the federal government forcibly instituted a tribal-council type of government for the Hopi in 1935, most of the Hopi villages have resisted such changes and still consider themselves independent, with their own elected or hereditary leaders. Yet the earlier "closed community" aspect of the Hopi reservation is gradually being eroded because of the death of the elders and because there is substantial out-marriage and out-work. As with many American Indian tribes, several Hopi ceremonies have been seriously weakened or lost entirely because of the death of the last elder who knew the correct form of the ceremony. Many Hopi have emigrated to the surrounding cities of Holbrook, Winslow, Flagstaff, Phoenix, Denver, and even as far away as San Francisco and New York City. The federal government's practice of sending teenagers to boarding schools off the reservation has naturally resulted in increased cross-cultural contact and marriage outside the tribe,

5. It is linguistically interesting that the Hopi tribe, though relatively small and confined to a fairly limited area, nevertheless has strong dialect differences among native speakers from different villages.

further weakening the tribal cultural fabric, including the Hopi language. However, the Hopi culture is still very much alive. The tribal council has established a Cultural Preservation Office, and tribal leaders are actively working to preserve cultural ways and to transmit to the younger Hopis an appreciation for traditional Hopi beliefs and practices.[6] There are now several government-supported predominantly Hopi elementary schools on the reservation, and Hopi students attend high school either on the reservation or in public or private schools off the reservation.

Edmund Nequatewa was born into the Sun Forehead Clan of the Hopi tribe in about 1880. His exact birth year is uncertain. There are discrepancies between nineteenth-century government records and verifiable dates, such as the building of a new school dormitory and dining hall at Keams Canyon in 1895 and the smallpox epidemic in 1898–99. This book is Edmund's own account of his youth in the Shipaulovi area, the strong influence of the grandfather who adopted him, his school-related experiences at Keams Canyon and in Phoenix, and his personal attempts to adjust to two different worlds.

The girl mentioned at the end of Edmund's account became his first wife, June, of the Cloud Clan at Shipaulovi. They settled at Shipaulovi and had three sons. Two subsequently died at the Phoenix Indian School, and Edmund and his wife then moved to Flagstaff so that the youngest son could attend public school there.

In Flagstaff, Edmund became one of the many Hopi employees the Museum of Northern Arizona hired over the years to perform

6. Those desiring more information about Hopi culture should first consult the excellent comprehensive annotated bibliography by W. David Laird, published by the University of Arizona Press in 1977. Those desiring more information about the Hopi language and its relationships should consult either my 1977 article, "Hopi Linguistics: An Annotated Research Bibliography," or the extensive bibliography at the end of my *Hopi dictionary.*

ordinary maintenance chores as well as to help in the museum's efforts at achieving wider understanding of and appreciation for Hopi
history and culture. It was at the museum that Edmund met Alfred
Whiting.[7] They became lifelong friends and often traveled to the
Hopi reservation together. Edmund eventually got into trouble at the
museum, however, and his employment there was terminated.

At about age sixty, Edmund and his first wife separated. He
married a Hopi woman named Jean from the village of Hotevilla on
Third Mesa. They lived at Hotevilla and had eight children. In his
continuing search for truth during his advanced years, Edmund
became associated with a Protestant splinter religious sect, and for a
while his home was the official meeting place of that group. He died
in Hotevilla on April 28, 1969, after a long illness.[8]

For well over a hundred years there has been a keen interest in
the oral literature and oral history of American Indians. Some
researchers have collected animal stories and myths, while others
have concentrated on recording the life histories of individuals
from various Indian tribes. More than a thousand life histories of
American Indians have been collected. These vary in length and
quality from brief tape recordings or a few handwritten notes to

7. Whiting's first professional job was as Curator of Biology at the Museum of
Northern Arizona, where he researched and wrote his *Ethnobotany of the Hopi*. After World War II he served for one year as a government anthropologist for
Ponape Island in the South Pacific. Later he became Curator for Anthropology at
the Dartmouth College Museum in Hanover, New Hampshire, returning fre-
quently to his beloved Southwest. In 1974 he retired to Arizona in hopes of revis-
ing his manuscript on the ethnobotany of the Hopi and completing other projects,
such as the Nequatewa biography. Unfortunately, Whiting contracted bone cancer
and died in May 1978 at the age of sixty-six. The more than 55,000 pages of his
ethnographic notes and papers now make up the Whiting Collection in the Special Collections and Archives Department of the Cline Library at Northern Arizona University in Flagstaff.

8. A brief obituary written by his former employer, Harold S. Colton, appears in
a 1969 issue of the Museum of Northern Arizona's *Plateau* magazine (no. 4, pp.
154–155).

printed works published privately or commercially. A decade ago David Brumble studied and annotated over five hundred such life histories, more than a hundred of which were of book length.[9] For the Hopi there are three well-known published biographies, all of Third Mesa people.[10] Edmund's story of his childhood now provides an authentic account from Second Mesa. \

Recently there has been increasing attention to both the content and the style of life histories.[11] Oral-history associations have sprung up, and many essays about interview and recording techniques have appeared.[12] Researchers have carefully scrutinized the relationship between the interviewer and the interviewee and are discussing guidelines for all aspects of the collection and preservation of life histories. Brumble and others have made the point that the majority of published accounts are shaped largely by Anglo recorders and editors who are intentionally or unintentionally responding to the perceived needs of a white audience. Much authenticity has thus been lost for the sake of correct grammar and similar ethnocentric factors. Nevertheless, the growing interest in what anthropologists and linguists call discourse analysis provides encouragement for us to produce more examples of authentic narration for American Indian autobiographies. Word lists are now considered of much less importance than the unique ways in which different peoples string together words into sentences, paragraphs, and longer utterances.

9. H. David Brumble III, *An Annotated bibliography of American Indian and Eskimo autobiographies* (1981).

10. These are Talayesva's *Sun chief* (1942), Qoyawayma's *No turning back* (1964), and Sekaquaptewa's *Me and mine* (1969).

11. One of the most knowledgeable discussions can be found in David Brumble's book, *American Indian autobiography* (1988), and in Greg Sarris' 1990 review of that book in the *American Indian Culture and Research Journal*.

12. For example, see James Clifford's *The Predicament of culture* (1988), several of the essays collected in Dunaway and Baum's book *Oral history* (1984), and both of David Brumble's books cited earlier.

The current intense academic study of human discourse in cultures around the world has helped to draw attention to the varieties of preliterate and literate self-expression among Native American peoples. Researchers have finally recognized that there are literary and cultural merits in providing narrative as close as possible to the original recording and that it is neither necessary nor desirable to edit away the nonwhite style used by a native speaker. The Hopi narrative style of English used by Edmund is largely unedited. Verb subjects and tenses, for example, often are not as the Anglo reader would expect them to be, yet they help illustrate Edmund's usage when he is telling a Hopi-oriented story from the past. The preservation of this unique narrative style is one of the important contributions of this book.

Edmund wanted his childhood story to be told. He sensed that it would be informative and interesting to Hopi and non-Hopi alike. In 1942, when Edmund was in his sixties, he asked his longtime friend Alfred Whiting to record the life story of his best Hopi friend. At the time, Whiting was getting ready to return to his graduate studies at the University of Chicago. Nevertheless, he quickly enlisted the aid of a local student named Sterling MacIntosh, and together the three men set out to record Edmund's memories of his childhood. As Whiting recounts:

> Somehow in the hectic weeks that followed we three found evenings in which Edmund talked, Sterling recorded, and I listened, interrupting only to stem the flow of too rapid speech, to clarify pronouns or to insist that Edmund talk for a general audience who could not be expected to know the things he himself had so diligently taught me over the preceding years.
>
> There was no plot. None of us, including Edmund, seemed to know what was coming next nor just what goal we might eventually reach. The strict scientific sanctity of the Museum

cast a taboo on the subject of sex. This was perhaps not without justification, for it was in this particular field of activity that Edmund's transgressions soon afterward led to his leaving the Museum staff. The end of our work came swiftly. Sterling dashed off the last of his copy and grabbed the train west. I struggled through a disastrous final week with Edmund by myself. I think we were all tired of the project by that time. He was rambling considerably. I made a valiant attempt to record a reasonably final scene and left town.

Whiting worked on his manuscript off and on for the next twenty years, occasionally conferring with his Hopi friend and informant, especially to clarify confusing names and dates in Edmund's early childhood. Understandably, Edmund's advancing age and diminishing memory made this task increasingly difficult. Whiting writes:

Shortly before Christmas in 1961, I had a very brief visit with Edmund, the first time I had seen him in many years. I read most of the manuscript to him. An attempt was made to establish the proper sequence of events in his early childhood. Nevertheless, I doubt the accuracy of the sequence of events as we have them recorded and the dates we have assigned to them.

The reader will readily recognize that the inexact dates of Edmund's story are not nearly as significant as the overall content of his firsthand account of Hopi Indian life at the end of the nineteenth century. The editorial policy here has been to remove confusing date references and to follow Whiting's wishes that Edmund's speech be left in its original special Hopi narrative style of spoken English.[13] In this book I have avoided changing any of Edmund's

13. See, for example, the language items under Voegelin and several other authors cited in David Laird's *Hopi bibliography*, and numerous Hopi language articles in such periodicals as the *International Journal of American Linguistics*.

words or expressions except where further clarification was absolutely essential. Indeed, the preservation of this style may be one of the most important and useful features of this book. Edmund's account is clearly a "Hopi voice" from the past, presented here as closely as possible to the original telling. The narrative style—even in its occasional awkwardness—is valuable in and of itself.

Fifty years after its initial recording, this Hopi story is even more cogent and timely than it was when it was first recorded. Given the current interest in discourse analysis, Edmund's account will provide abundant material for comparisons with life histories from other American Indian cultures as well as from other cultures around the world. As final editor, I believe this book will honor the Hopi people as well as their good friend Al Whiting. I gladly identify with the final statement in Whiting's original manuscript preface: "The story that follows is Edmund's, and all the errors are mine."

P. DAVID SEAMAN
Northern Arizona University

 Autobiography

Kachina

My name is Edmund. This is my own story, the best I can remember, from my boyhood teachings and experiences.

When you first begin to remember, then you begin to realize that the presents are given to you by the Kachina. And then someone will be telling you that these Kachina come from the underworld and that they go into the underworld through the kivas in the villages, or they fly to the San Francisco Peaks to go into the underworld. They are supposed to form wings just before they leave the Hopi village. The wings would replace the arms. Each person that dies goes into the underworld, and if they want to return, they return as Kachina, male or female. If they don't return as Kachina, they will follow the Kachina as clouds because they are spirits.[14]

Then you don't know; there are a lot of hard things to explain. If you had some of your loved ones die recently, just before the Kachina come to dance, you are precautioned not to shed any

---

14. Much has been published about Hopi religion. Informed and sympathetic treatments include John Loftin's dissertation, "Emergence and ecology" (1983) and his *Religion and Hopi life in the Twentieth Century* (1991).

tears. As I remember, the oldest daughter of my mother's parents died. My grandfather and grandmother were told by the brother of the girl that died not to shed any tears. "Father and Mother, by all means do not shed any tears because we like to have sister enjoy the dance if she comes with the rest of the clouds to view the dance. Otherwise, if you do cry you will let her suffer."

So everyone would at least try not to ever shed any tears, no matter how many of their loved ones had passed away, because any Kachina dance is for all the people on the face of the earth, and also for the dead because it is sure they will come to see the dance as clouds.

When I was a small child I would know the Kachinas are coming about a day or two ahead of time, because the people would be preparing; everyone would be busy. My mother and the rest of the women would be grinding corn to make piki or to prepare for the feast.[15] My father would go after mutton, and I will be sure when the mutton is brought and butchered. They would not butcher mutton except on a very special occasion.

Just as soon as you found out that the dance is going to be held, you are always warned. My parents would say, "Now, you must be as good as you can to receive any presents from the Kachina. But if you're going to be naughty like you always have been, you are not going to expect to see any presents."

I would say, "What kind of presents?"

"Well, I don't know. I would never know the kind of presents you are going to receive. I'm not the one to bring you presents. It will be the Kachina that bring you presents."

---

15. Cornmeal forms the basis of many special Hopi dishes, by far the most popular of which is Hopi wafer bread, or *piki*. Piki is made from a thin batter of cornmeal, usually hand ground from blue corn and mixed with ashes of the saltbush or bean vine to keep the batter alkaline. Piki is cooked on a thin stone griddle and is then peeled off as a large, thin, flexible sheet, which is quickly folded and rolled like a newspaper. It is prepared in quantity before important Hopi ceremonies and is often served to guests when a regular meal is not being served.

The day before the dance, the women would be very busy. Everybody would be making piki all day long. Just as soon as the sun goes down, the big pots would be on the fireplace.

After the day was over, mother had made some pikis and had them put away in the piki closet. The piki closet was usually in the corner someplace built out of a cedarwood frame, with slabs of flagstone. These small cedars would be put into the wall in the corner and would be crossed at right angles. The shelves would be made out of sunflower stalks and were plastered over inside and outside. For a door there will be a little blanket hanging over the door, a white blanket, or women's shawl for over their shoulders. The walls would be either cedar or sunflower stalk or flagstone. It was always sunflower stalks in our house. Shelves were plastered over with white plaster, and so were the walls. The piki closet was always about four or five feet off from the floor and reaching up to the ceiling. There might be a water storage jar under it. Whether they realized the idea or not, the water being evaporated right under the piki closet kept the pikis nice and moist. The water jar was covered with a slab of stone. The lids for cooking pots or any other pots were all stones.

After my mother had been making piki all day, she started washing her hominy which she had made, boiling it with ashes. She would use white corn and wood ashes of sagebrush wood and boil it about three hours. She had it boiling while she was making piki. She was making piki right out on the porch where she had her piki stone, on the second floor. This porch had a roof over it. She had the hominy setting by the fireplace after it was done. The fireplace is in the house in the corner, in the same room where the piki closet was. The pot was one of those Hopi cooking pots, one that she made. It was cooling off beside the fire. After she got through washing it, it was then ready. She uses the water that Father had been bringing up from the spring about one mile and a half on the west side of the mesa, carrying the old water jar on his back, one jar at a time. The jar has pottery handles and a tumpline braided out of cowhide and wool yarn. The strap that goes over the head is about two inches wide and about ten inches long, going down to the jar. The wool part goes clear through the pottery loops and is tied to the water jug with the knot between his back and the pot, at the bottom of the pot, which also helps to hold up the jar.

When father came up the ladder, mother looked out through the door and saw him coming and says, "Bring the water over here and set it here so I could use it to wash this hominy, so I won't have to use any more which you have already brought and put in the storage jar."

"All right, here you are," he said, setting it there. "If there isn't enough water yet, I might go after some more."

"We have plenty of water now. You have been carrying water all day long, and I think it's time you rest for a while and cut up the meat for the stew. I have a pot on the fireplace, and just as soon as it comes to a boil, put the meat in."

It was on the same fire. I was right there because it was getting dark. And when the water comes to a boil, mother asked father to cut up the meat, which is usually—just about always—the backbone of the mutton. Might be some of the front quarter with it. After the meat was all cut, mother put that in the pot where the water was boiling. Just as soon as the meat got cooked enough, she put in her hominy. Just about that time mother asked me to go to bed.

"Son, it is time for you to go to bed. If you do go to bed now, about toward morning I'll let you know when the Kachina come, so that you may hear them."

I did know that the Kachina do come to the plaza early in the morning, around about 3:00 in the morning, to go through the rehearsal in the plaza. So along about that time in the morning, they did come. So mother crawled over where I was and says, "Wake up and listen. The Kachina are here."

Instead of opening my eyes, I just jumped right up out of the bed and started for the door. Father got out of bed and ran after me and says to me at the door, "Don't go out there and see those Kachina. No one is supposed to see the Kachina at this time of morning. Anyone that sees the Kachina when they are in the plaza at this time of morning will be charmed and some sort of calamity will befall him. Sometimes these sores will break out on your face. You can only listen, but you cannot see them until they come again after sunrise."

I went back to bed and I listened and I heard them dancing in the plaza. Finally I heard an old man yelling sort of an urging or encouraging speech to the Kachina. After the dance was over, the man said, "I am glad that I have found you here. Since I have found you I will hold you for a day after the sun comes up. So I will only send you back to the Kachina resting place, then you can come back again when the sun comes up. That is all I am going to say until you come back again, and then I will tell you something else."

While the old man was talking, a Kachina would answer him with his rattler. It is a gourd rattle, and as he answers he shakes that a very vigorous shake. Every time the man would pause, the rattles would go. Just one would answer; he is supposed to be the song leader. I heard all that and then gone back to sleep again.

About dawn, my mother woke me up again. "Wake up, it's time to get up and you must go out with your sacred corn and ask for your blessing, and also ask that the Kachina would bring you some presents."

So I got right up and got ready. I got up and threw my old rabbitskin blanket back off the sheepskin, and then I went over where my bell usually hangs on a hook or a stick and put it around my waist. In those days they were those Spanish bells of some kind. Earlier they were pottery bells. But now they were more like copper sheep bells or something like that. I put it around my waist and started out just outside of the village where there was a shrine, because I wasn't anxious to go off anywhere. The bell hung down on my hip. In those days, you know, a boy wasn't supposed to wear any G-string until after he received his first kilt. I must be about six or seven. I went down the ladder facing the ladder. All the older people would walk down facing away from the ladder. I ran out about fifty yards around the village where there was the first shrine. I just held my hand up to my mouth. The sacred corn was kept on the mantle, and I held it in my closed fist. I just held it in my closed fist with the palm up. You are supposed to say something. Of course, at that age you can't very well say what you want to ask for. You just let a long breath out on it and bring it down, with your palm down, and sprinkle it toward the rising sun.

I run back to the house. When I got up the ladder and went into the house and took my bell off and put it back on the peg, I saw mother was making this lather of soapsuds out of the soapweed. When she gets through then, she asks father to come over and lean over into the bowl.

"It is done. You come over and undo your hair and lean over into the bowl so I will wash your head."

So father undid his hair. To undo his hair he untied it, which was in a knot on the back of his head. It was always tied with a white wool cord. My father had an awful lot of hair, sort of reddish brown. His hair must be about two and a half feet long, down below his waist.

He came over there and leaned over the pot and mother took his hair and flopped it over his head, and his hair almost filled up the bowl. After she was done washing his hair, then mother untied her hair. It was in rolls on both sides of her head. She had a lot of hair. Each roll on the side of her head must be about close to two inches and a half diameter, about as big as her forearm. It was tied with a human hair cord made of someone else's hair. This hair cord would be one of her wedding presents. She washed her head, and when she got through she said, "Now, Son, it is your turn to wash your hair."

"It's too cold. I don't want to wash my head."

"If you're going to get any presents, you have to wash your head. No child will ever receive any presents from the Kachina if they have a dirty head like you. After you wash your hair, I will comb it so you will become a very handsome boy."

I didn't want to wash my hair, so she went and called one of my uncles, her brother. He came over there. Just as soon as he came into the house he picked me up and just held me with my arms, and I was kicking around, making a big fuss. He got me so I just can't do anything and put my head in the bowl, and mother washed my hair. My hair was so fuzzy. After that I was so mad I just rolled right down in the trash pile where my mother had it piled by the door. Then my mother called the uncle back again. He picked me up and put my head back into the bowl again. He was about eighteen or twenty. Before he let me go he says, "If you do it again, I will come back every time no matter how much water we waste, every time you put your head into the dirt." This uncle of mine down in Phoenix still makes fun of me for that. Every time when they washed my head I ran for the trash pile.

Then finally I got my head clean, and mother wrapped me up in my wearing blanket and set me beside the fire, because I was crying all this time. So finally I get warmed up. We were ready to eat by this time. Mother set the table on the floor. She cleared a space on the floor, sweeping it off with a brush broom that also was the hair brush and got the piki on the Havasupai basket tray. She got the mutton stew and put it in a decorated bowl, one that she got from the Walapai people who live near the Grand Canyon, and salt from the salt lake forty miles south of Zuni. Father had gone for it.

While we were eating, the Kachina had come and started dancing in the plaza. I got right up and started out for the plaza. When I got out there I found that this was Niman Kachina, and they just have armfuls of green corn on the stalks, and they have been laid right in the plaza, and the Kachina were dancing. Each child must be wishing for the presents they will receive. We hadn't had any green corn before then. All that corn, and then melons that my two hands could just cover. They had been still green, but they were important in this dance. No one was supposed to know anything about what these Kachina would bring, because they were supposed to be the only ones that would have early crops. These they really prepare for the children as gifts.

The Kachina look like angels. There were a line of Kachina, must be around about twenty-five of them in a line, dancing. They had wonderful costumes on, and kilts and sashes, and over that these long Douglas fir boughs, and also they have the same kind of firs around their necks. Their bodies were painted black. Their heads and faces were painted with at least five colors: green, yellow, red, black, and blue.

I had seen them, but this was the first particular time that I ever did notice. I was watching them very carefully. They also have a tall headdress on. It must be about two feet tall, above their heads, and some feathers on it. I wondered just how they were put on there, and I thought each of the rest of the kids were wondering the same as I was doing, but I didn't ask anyone. The rest may be as scared as I am, but no one would say anything about it.

After they got through dancing, they started to pick up the corn that they had laid down, and after they got it in their arms, they went around looking for their friends, kids they were supposed to make friends with if they give them the presents. As though this was sort of a punishment, most of the rest of the children have received their presents and there I was sitting right up against the house in the plaza. After a long while, this one Kachina was walking around and couldn't seem to find a friend, and there I was wishing that it was for me. At last he walked up to me and gave me this bunch of corn. I felt so happy I almost cried to think that I had been naughty that morning.

Just as soon as I received my present I ran home, and when I got to the ladder I couldn't get up, so I called to mother and she came down and helped me up with my presents. When we get into the house, she says to place them up in the corner and sprinkle some sacred cornmeal over them and then go back to the plaza and hide away from these presents, and when I come back I may find them increased. So, after doing that, I went back to the plaza. I wanted to go right back as soon as I can to see what had happened. So I ran back to the house and climbed up the ladder, and I went into the room, and mother was still there. Just as soon as I got in I asked her if she had a look at the presents.

"Mother, have you looked at the presents and see if there is any more than what I had left there?"

She says, "No, that would be for you to go back and look at it. Since you have been naughty this morning, I am afraid there won't be any more than what you had left there." So, to make sure, I went over into the corner and looked, and there was still just as much as I had left there. Mother says, "Is there any more there?"

I said, "No." I felt like crying.

Mother said, "You go hide again. You have been naughty, and when you come back maybe you will see that the Kachina brought you some more presents."

I went back again to watch the dance some more. This time I stayed a little longer. When I went back, just as soon as I got in through the door I went straight for the corner where the presents were. This time I found a big pile of green corn. Mother felt very happy. Mother went right to work and put the pot on the fireplace, with water in it, and she took some of this corn and put it in to boil. She didn't take the husks off, but it would come off when the corn was done. These corns were the presents to the children, and the parents were not supposed to eat any of it until the child got enough, or had the first taste of it.

The dance was on all day. At noontime they begin to bring in some more presents—bows and arrows and dolls. The boys would receive the bows and arrows, and the girls would receive the dolls.

During all day I would be noticing all their movements. When one of these Kachina came up to me and handed me the bows and arrows, and bent down and I was looking up, I saw the light clear across the eyes through the mask. I also looked at the mouth, and it was just a little slit. I wondered how they would eat and how they would drink water, because the rolls of piki are too big, and they have just a little mouth. I went and asked my mother how did the Kachina eat.

"Well, why?" she says.

"Because the Kachina have only a little bit of a mouth."

"But their mouths stretch just like yours."

So I didn't say any more, because I supposed that she does know that they really do stretch. But I just can't get that thing out of my head—seeing the light through the eyes. It was the first time I got any suspicious ideas.

2

Born a Chief

Now there was something else I did not know at first. We were living in Mishongnovi[16] and I always thought that was where I was born. But one day I learned that this was not the way it had been. Later I found out all about it, and now I will tell you some history so you will understand.

In the early days there were only two villages on Second Mesa, Mishongnovi and Shungopovi. Each village had its own series of ceremonies. Each ceremony was put on by a society, a group of men who met in a special ceremonial room built underground, called a _kiva_. Now each kiva and the society that met there was in the care of a different clan, and the head of that society was selected from that clan, usually from some particular family within that clan.

In the year of 1680 the chief of Shungopovi was worried.[17] His village had been active in the revolt that year in which the Hopi and the Pueblo Indians of New Mexico had thrown out the Spaniards

16. See the brief geographical sketch in the introduction and the map of northeastern Arizona above.

17. There are several published versions of the historical account that Edmund relates here. Naturally, this one parallels that contained in his book _Truth of a Hopi_ (1936).

and killed the missionary priests. The Spaniards had returned to New Mexico, and it was expected that they would soon return to the Hopi towns as well. The chief was very worried for fear the Spaniards would destroy his village and that the rituals held every year for the benefit of all the people in the world would stop.

The chief selected a family from each of the clans who were responsible for the religious ceremonies. These families were to go to a place called Shipaulovi and build homes there. This was near enough to Mishongnovi to provide some protection. Each family then could carry on the rituals which were threatened at Shungopovi, and in case the Spaniards did come back to get revenge, the Shungopovi could claim that the new town at Shipaulovi was innocent.

Since the Bear Clan people were at that time always the head of the towns in the Hopi country, then of course the Bear Clan must be the head of this new town also. The brother of the chief of Shungopovi was the man appointed by his brother to be the Shipaulovi chief, but only a subchief, as he would still be under his Shungopovi brother. The subchief was told that he must attend all the ceremonies over at Shungopovi first before he carries out his own ceremonies at Shipaulovi. This is how Shipaulovi had its start.

After everything was pretty well established, the chief of Shungopovi went and told his brother that in case the Spaniards should come, whom he was looking for all this time, they might put Shungopovi into ruins, that he and his Shungopovi people may be no more, and that his Shipaulovi brother would then inherit everything—that is, the land—and will call it his own, for he will be the only one to have the right to claim it. It was understood that if the old chief's town of Shungopovi should not be altogether destroyed, that if any of his people should survive, then the Shungopovi people would, of course, still have a right to the property they owned.

It was not until after twenty years that the Spaniards did come. Instead of going right up into the town, they made camp about a mile below the town. From there they sent word up to the Shungopovi chief to come. The chief came down with his bodyguards or braves and was asked if he would sacrifice a hundred of his people for the crime of killing the Spanish missionaries. If the chief agreed, his own life would be spared. If not, his whole town would be put in ruins, and no one would be spared. Then, of course, the chief would not give up too many innocent people, for he knew exactly who the men were who were involved in the rebellion.

All this time the chief himself did not know that he was being taken captive, so he sent word back up to Shungopovi for the men to come whom he had named, so these men had to come because it was their own chief who had asked them to come. When these men went down to the place, quite a number of the rest of the men went with them. They were then all taken as prisoners. An argument was then started among themselves, and it was found that this rebellion was the fault of the chief's people, who were the Bear Clan. The Hopi could not decide then what should be done to save some of the young men. Just then, one of the Strap Clan men stepped forward and said that he himself objected and that the young men should not be taken prisoners or killed for the sake of the old chief. Then everybody said that if the chief should insist that those who were taken prisoners would be killed, that he should not be respected as a chief of his people. The chief said that he could do nothing else because he had already given up these men. Then the Strap Clan man said that the old chief had no heart for himself and his people, so then he was asked to be chief no more. The Strap Clan man was chosen as the leader and chief. So, hesitating no more, he stepped forward up to the prisoners and picked out the young men who he knew still had a good many more years to live and started homeward with these men and left the chief and the rest of the prisoners with the Spaniards.

The next morning the prisoners were shot at sunrise, and there were a hundred of them. The Spaniards did this and left them, and the people from Shungopovi came down and buried them.

The Spaniards were seen no more at that place. The Hopis were always in fear of them from then on. For that reason they moved their villages up on top of the mesa. Even moving up on top of the mesa, they were not sure of safety, and for that reason there were at that time no trails where the Spaniards might come up. They would have animal trails and a foot trail. The foot trails were only toe holds on the side of the cliffs in those days. They had very difficult foot trails with these toe holds but nothing that a person could just walk up. At the top of these trails there was always a pile of big rocks. This was a means of defense.

The new town of Shipaulovi gradually got pretty well established, and the population was growing quite well. It was not so very many years before they were building many houses and spreading out on the west side. All the troubles with the Spaniards were forgotten and the people were quite prosperous. Then there was an epidemic of smallpox. This, of course, took most of the people at all the towns of the Hopi country. There were so few people left on Second Mesa that for a while the complete service of annual ceremonies was only held at Shungopovi.

Times gradually improved, and after some years Shipaulovi carried on all its own ceremonies, and the village became truly independent. However, the population was small, and often in the particular family responsible for some ceremonies there would not be women whose sons could continue the ceremonies. Then some other closely related family in the same or an allied clan would have to assume the responsibility. So when they first moved to Shipaulovi, the Crane Clan, who was responsible for the One Horned Society, built a house with a special room in which to keep the altar and other ritual objects used in their ceremonies.[18]

The time came when there were only two old men left in that

18. Although Edmund refers to the One Horned Society or the One Horned Fraternity, which occupies the Agave Kiva, throughout much of the literature on the Hopi it is referred to as the Agave Society.

clan, and they realized that if they died, the ceremonies would be lost. A family of the Sun Forehead Clan volunteered to carry on the responsibility, and they did this for a number of years after the death of the One Horned men. Then when the last Sun Forehead man was getting old, there was no woman in his family who could provide a son who could be trained to carry on the ceremonies after he had died, so he brought up this question again among the members of the society. Of course, it made everyone sick at heart. But their wishes were that their ceremonial rites should not be lost. So it was decided that another family of the same clan should be given the responsibility.

There were a number of girls in this family, and the next to the oldest girl was chosen to inherit the Crane Clan house. She was at that time only about ten years old, but it was agreed that if she should ever marry and raise a family, the first-born son should inherit the chieftainship of the One Horned Society. That girl was my mother.

There was another branch of the same family who thought that they should have been selected, and they were very jealous. When mother got married and moved into the Crane Clan house, they would pester her and come up to her and scold her for no reason at all, only to make her feel bad.

Three years after moving into that house, the chosen girl had a son. The grandmother—the father's mother—named him Edmund. According to the original plan, he would become the head chief of the One Horned Society. That was me.

This birth made the other family more jealous, and they pestered my mother even more. She felt that she could bear this trouble no longer, so my father decided that we should move over to his family's home in Mishongnovi.[19] So one night, without saying a

19. In the traditional matrilocal Hopi society, such a move would be quite unusual and would ordinarily occur only after social infighting became intolerable.

Clan house inheritance:
   chieftainships of societies & clans.

word to anyone, we went over to my father's home and lived there for a number of years, as I have described.

There in Mishongnovi is where I begin to remember that I was alive, and as I said before, I didn't know that I really belonged in the Crane Clan house in Shipaulovi.

3

Growing and Building
In Mishongnovi

After moving to Mishongnovi, my family felt much happier. The boy was then old enough to be around with the rest of the children on the streets, with his bows and arrows, playing games with the sticks, or sometimes the crowd of them might be playing shinney ball in the plaza.[20]

You know, there was this uncle of mine, who lives in Phoenix now, my father's brother. Him and Vivian, my aunt, and another cousin, we used to play together. The girls would be grinding corn, and we would pretend that we were out hunting. They would be cooking and making piki. We would pretend relationships from real life.

One time some other children from another family started playing with us. This uncle of mine was supposed to get married. This girl came to our "house" we had divided up in a room. She came and

20. In shinney ball, a buckskin ball stuffed with wool is buried in a dirt mound in the center of the playing field, with brush houses built for goals at either end of the field. No one is allowed to touch the ball with his hands. Two captains face off at the dirt mound, and each beats at the mound with a stick until the ball is uncovered. Then it is hit to teammates, who use sticks to try to hit the ball into their team's goal while the other team uses sticks to try to capture the ball and drive it into their own goal at the opposite end of the field.

got married. We pretended that we would go out and get some firewood, and we would go down to the kiva and make her wedding robe. It would be a piece of muslin or something like that. She would be making piki. Then, of course, we had to finish the robe, and we sent the girl home with her robe. The groom, of course, has to wait until he gets his gift of corn from the bride. This took place in Mishongnovi at my grandfather's. I don't remember much about those early days.

As I got older I had to take care of the sheep and help in the fields. At planting time they would dig the holes in the field, and I would come along and put the seeds into the holes and cover them up. By this time I had quit playing with the girls, as it would be considered sissy. Boys and girls do play together. But just as soon as the boy gets old enough, it would be rather sissy for him to play with the girls, and the boys are supposed to be out in the field and not playing with the girls. Boys don't like to be called a sissy, so they don't play with the girls or even seem to like the girls.

In the summertime when the planting season is on, a boy would do nothing but herd sheep and many other things that he was taught besides attending to the flock of sheep. In his early days the Hopi boy must learn to hunt, learn to use his bow and arrows, and also the throwing of sticks. All this I had to learn.

When the crops in the summertime are pretty well on their way, I would be out in the fields watching or guarding the crops so that nothing might hurt the corn or watermelons. One summer I was watching the crops when the watermelons were quite green. I had been wishing that the melons were ripe enough so that I could have one. I spotted a fine watermelon and then walked back about fifty yards and took a shot at it. Of course, if you shoot the melon, then you have to pick it! Father came along just then, and I told him that I was shooting at a lizard. He said, "It is too bad that you accidentally shot this melon when you were shooting at a lizard. It is all right this time, but don't do it again, for it's such a waste." But of course I didn't waste it!

Sometimes a number of us boys guarded the fields in summer together. We hunted rabbits or anything we could find. This was usually lizards or horned toads. But if they are playing that they are older and out on a big hunt, we would be after bear or antelope. They would ride sticks to pretend they were on horseback. The horses were not named. Sometimes they would have a string for a rein. We ran races on the stick horses. If we are pretending that we are horse racing, we would usually be gambling. Two boys would want to race, but they would pretend that the sticks were horses. They would divide up, and they would bet on a certain horse rather than a rider. They will pretend that one party is from some other village. It is usually Walpi people, as they were the great gamblers. They would do this quite often, but it would all depend on how good horses they have. After the crop was ripe, they would bet so many ears of corn, but if that was not ripe, they would bet their arrows. The most valuable thing they have was their arrows.

Sometimes your parents might object. "Those arrows were given to you by the Kachina. If you are losing all your arrows by betting, the Kachina will not bring you any more." But the parents would not keep the boy from betting his arrows. They would just scold him; they know they will have to make him arrows no matter how bad he might be.

If I lost in a game, I would sneak into the house and steal one of my own arrows. I would have a bunch of old arrows, and I would stick the new one into the middle of the old ones as I carried it out, for fear that my mother and father would see that I was taking the new one. My mother would usually notice anyway.

"Where are you going with that arrow?"

"What arrow?"

"Didn't you just get one of your new ones out?"

"No." I would hold up my arrows.

She would come over. "Just let me see."

And then I would run for the ladder, throw my arrows down off the roof, and then climb down to them and pick them up and run off. My arrows had always been carefully counted. If mother really did see that I was taking out a new arrow along with my old ones, she would go back and count my new ones, and then she would know if one was missing and if I had taken a new arrow.

When I got back at night, father and mother would always give me a good talking-to. They would not say anything to me until after I had eaten my supper, for fear that I would get mad and not eat. My mother would say, "Son, I found that you had taken one of your arrows out of your new ones. And I suppose that you did not bring it back. You had lost that in the game. Those arrows will not last very long if you keep on gambling."

Then my father would join her and say, "Well, it is quite a long ways yet before the Kachina who gave you those arrows will come around here again. Of course, I can make arrows, but I can never paint them with such colors as the Kachina use, because I have none. And I don't know how to make such colors."

I didn't realize we were planning to build a house at first, but later on my dad was carrying up some rocks, and I asked him what he was doing with them. He said he is going to build a house. In carrying them, he had a sheepskin on his back with a wide part for the rock to lay in so he wouldn't hurt himself lifting the rocks. We got the rocks on the north side of Mishongnovi. We didn't have any big stone hammer, but he used some of the old axes. Sometimes mother would help him and they would carry rocks up all day long. They had quite a pile.

The plan was just to be a two-room house.[21] In those days the

21. Here Edmund is describing an ordinary house building in Mishongnovi. The clan house in Shipaulovi was more elaborate, as he describes in Chapter 5.

largest room would be about ten by twelve. The beams would be long enough to reach across a ten-foot space. We had gotten the beams from grandfather's cottonwood trees. In those days they planted cottonwood trees for that purpose, to get the beams from. The men do this in their own fields. They transplant them in the month of March while the ground is wet, taking a green shoot. They trim them back and leave a few branches toward the top and keep the branches off of the bottom. This was to keep them growing straight in order to use them for beams in the future. Now they don't use them for beams anymore.

The way these logs were dragged up was by burro. The burro would have a saddle on, and two logs would be tied together at the butt end, or larger end. They will tie a strap around them about eighteen inches between the logs, doubled maybe twice. It takes two men to load them. Each will lift up the log and put it up from the back side of the burro. They will put the strap right over the front saddle horn. Then they will have to put another strap around the burro's neck to keep the saddle in place so it will not slide back off the burro. There might be two or three burros dragging the logs at once. They would get to the foot of the mesa, and then those burros sure had to pull! The logs are strapped, too, right under the middle of the burro's back, so if one log should happen to swing clear out, they will kind of keep together. There is another strap back of the saddle that acts as a guide for the two logs.

We brought twelve logs because we had to have two rooms. We cut the trees down with a steel axe. We had to let the logs season. They would be cut for one year.

The house was supposed to be just one story, with doors on the outside. They laid the foundation, and it must be about four feet high. There were no windows; there might be a ventilator, that's all. It would be down at the bottom of the wall. It is about ten inches by ten inches. It would be just open; that's the way all the ventilators were in those days. There would be a ventilator for each room.

There would be a doorway but no door. If there is going to be any door, there would be just a rabbitskin blanket hanging there. There is going to be a passageway between the two rooms, but only one outside door.

There would be no opening in the roof, only the chimney for the fireplace in both rooms. They would be in the corners. There would be a smokestack built there about two feet high, and then on it would be a pot with no bottom in it. If they wanted to make a chimney out of these pots, they have to take the bottom out. All the Hopi used to make their own pottery. My mother would have laid out a pot or two for this purpose by this time.

Then we got some beams about two or three inches in diameter. We got lots of these little fellows to use as crossbeams. We got them up in the cedars near the village. We would have to get them green so we can peel them off. We would get them about spring when the sap would be getting back into the tree. That is when the bark peels right off. They were about four or five feet long to be sure they will reach across.

In those days they would not be so particular. If they got a long piece, they don't cut it. The big beams would go out of the wall; that's for the purpose of hanging the skins and stretching them. They did this in the old houses. If the logs are not long enough to stick out, they will splice it so there will be something sticking out. There was wood across the top of the door.

Mortar is used, and when there is a working party on a house to lay stones, the women would first go out and get their sand and clay. Each woman goes out and gets her own, and then they go out after their own water. Then each woman would mix her mortar. All the houses were built like that.

I remember we had a working party for the first four feet of the wall. The town crier would call out the night before. He'll say, "Such and such a person is going to have a work party on a house, laying stone. All who wish, that would want to do the work or can spare their time, may come." Then whoever is able to spare their time come around very early. While the women get the mortar ready, the men make four or five trips down after rocks. When the mortar is ready, then they start laying stone, and they will kind of divide up around the wall. They will just draw a line or mark with their foot where the wall is supposed to be. First they step off so many steps the width and length of the rooms. They don't drive any stakes; they just make a little mark. They have to have a straight eye to drag his feet from one corner to the other.

The cornerstones would have a prayer plume.[22] So on each corner the stones are laid, and then on it the prayer plume is stuck with this sticky cactus sap. It might be a hawk feather or turkey feather. It is just a short feather, which has to be attached with string, about three or four inches of cotton string doubled four times and tied to it. It was believed that by doing this the house will stand forever.

The house is outlined when the gang gets there that morning. The outline would be made for the house. The corners would not be laid when they got there. Then, in order to lay the cornerstones, they will pick out the good-sized heavy ones. The man that is building the house will pick out these stones. If it is too heavy, it takes two men to handle it. The man that is building the house has to go out and get the cactus for the sticky sap. He would have done this beforehand, and early in the morning he would make the prayer plumes so that everything would be ready.

Then the rest would be working in between the corners. Each woman would pick out a section of the wall to work on. They will be putting on the stones and rocks. The men bring the rocks up and

22. Prayer plumes, or *pahos,* are string-and-feather combinations of infinite variety, often attached to objects of ceremonial significance. In its simplest form, a paho consists of a single feather attached to a homespun cotton thread. In more complex forms, Hopi pahos may involve several feathers, one or two sticks, and other symbolic additions.

wait there until the woman makes her mortar there, and then the man would put it up. Both of them watch to keep the wall straight. Husband and wife do not work together. The men will bring up stones whenever they are needed. The women would pile up their mortar high in one place, usually inside the wall. They would work either outside the wall or inside. The wall would be eight to ten inches thick, or one stone thick. Of course, they have to put these little pieces of stone in between the big ones with the mortar so that they get the big ones straight.

They will have to have lunch at noon. The man that is building the house provides lunch. In the evening they have a regular feast, either a bean feast or mutton stew. Everybody that works in the party would come to the feast. They would hold the feast at the old house of the person who was building the new house. It was only the well-to-do people who would have mutton stew for the working party in those days. Things were pretty scarce. My father and grandfather always had sheep, so they would have a mutton stew.

Maybe it was almost a month later that my uncles came over to help. My folks had done no more on the house, and they would have another working party instead of finishing it themselves. In those days people were very generous in that way. Nowadays they don't, unless you have cash to pay your man who comes to work for you. Sometimes a man might be working on his house, and then somebody would come up and, without saying a word, start in to help him. Another man might do the same thing until several were working on the house. Then the man who was building the house would send word down to his wife to get something ready for lunch. They would just give them lunch if they came to work like that, and the men had the privilege of leaving when they pleased if they had something else to do.

When it is finished, when the roof is put on, they always offer some food material that would be laid in the roof. They would have these roof beams and on top a lot of brush of sumac or willow, and then grass is laid on top of that about a foot thick. Then on top, someplace on the roof, they laid some piki, and then the mortar laid on top of the grass. They would fill the whole roof with real wet mortar because when that dried off on top of the grass, it makes the roof about one foot thick. After all the roof and everything is finished, then just before anyone touches the food that is being saved for the party, then another piece of piki, with a piece of stew meat rolled in it, is stuck in the roof in the ceiling, then a prayer plume, like the first one laid with the cornerstones. This time it will be on a stick in the ceiling, a single prayer plume on one stick. This would be done by the owner of the house.

Then the walls would just be the bare stones, so a working party might be held for plastering the walls. The women would do all the plastering. This time each woman had a separate pile of mortar for herself. When they got through with this mortar, they were through for the day. If someone had something else to do, they would come early and get the mortar up and then come back for the feast.

4

Initiation at Shipaulovi

One morning not long before the Bean Dance, I was down at the corral, helping father milk the goats. We had gone down early in the morning, and now I had a good can full of milk ready to take home.

When I got home, there was a stranger in the house, and I could tell that my mother had been crying. I put my milk away. My mother was just starting to put the pot on the fire. I sat down beside her and asked her what was wrong. All of a sudden she burst into tears and said, "Son, we have to go home."

"Home?" I said. There was no other place that was home to me. She said, "Yes, home to Shipaulovi."

I said, "Shipaulovi! I don't want to go there."

"We have to go. He says so. He is your uncle, and when he comes for us, we have to go."

In those days, you must remember, the mother's brother was the head of the family and had to be respected. He was always consulted when any trouble came up.

My mother had the milk boiling by then. She put in some corn-meal and made a gravy, which we drank. After this breakfast, mother packed her shelled corn—there must have been about fifty pounds—and we went over to Shipaulovi.

When we got on top of the mesa, we went over to my aunt's.[23] As soon as we got up there to the house, they both cried to their hearts' content. After everything was over, my mother asked if she should start the fire going under the piki stone. Then she has everything going, and mother went and started mixing piki. Both of the sisters, they make piki all day. That evening we went back to Mishongnovi. We spent the night over there.

The next morning we went back again, and that morning we took some of our bedding. My mother asked my father to bring some more of our bedding in the evening. That day was a big day. They didn't tell me I was to be initiated because they thought I would run away.

Along about evening, I noticed everybody was busy. Some man came in and I was in the house. My mother said to me, "There's your blanket over there. You take your blanket and put your moccasins on, and that man will take you to the kiva."

"What for?"

"Oh, the Kachina are coming and you're going to see them over there. It will be nice for you to see the Kachina, but go on now and go with the man."

The man said, "Come on and I will carry you on my back."

I thought it was fun to take a ride, so I put my moccasins on. A Hopi kid would be always wearing the same shirt. It was kind of dirty, but that didn't make any difference. I got on the man's back.

He got me almost to the ladder and let me off. I went in there and stepped around to the left side, and he went around on the right side.

23. For Edmund and his family to have been living at the paternal grandfather's house in Mishongnovi was not normal Hopi practice. Hopi sisters have a very close relationship, and this return to his mother's sister's house would be a move toward restoring normalcy.

I was about the last one that got in there. Finally we heard the foot-steps coming, up around the kiva roof. The man at the fireplace says, "Come in, we are waiting for you. We have been looking for you."

In come the Kachina. Two of them got into the center. Right in the center of the kiva is a big sand painting of this Kachina, and when they came in they looked like that. Then the argument started. This Kachina asked the man why he has been calling for them, why he has sent for them. The man said, "Well, we'd like to have these young people initiated, that they may learn about you, that you are the mythical gods, that you are our respected gods. That is the reason I had called for you." So the Mother Kachina looked around, and I see two Kachina with cholla cactus whips in both hands. The man said, "What you going to use those for? My children aren't that bad. They haven't done anything yet. I don't think you better use that."

"We have to. That is what we brought these for, to use on your children." Every child just sank and started crying, but I just looked on. I wondered if they were really going to use that. They argued back and forth just like that for a long time. Then the Mother Kachina says, "If they will promise that they will be good and respect us as their gods and your gods, we will do as you asked us."

The man says, "If they are going to have to promise all that, I'm the one that promises you. They are scared, they can't say all that. We are all going to be good and respect you as our gods. So as long as you said that you are going to take my word, here it is."

All this time a big bunch of yucca was in front of him, and the boys were between the legs of the godfathers and the girls with their godmothers. They took the cactus away from the Kachina and laid it beside the fireplace. Then these men handed this bunch of yucca to the Kachina, and both of the Kachina jumped on the sand painting and run all over it, just like putting it out of sight. They sat there, and then they said, "Who shall we take first?"

This man got up and said, "To prove that my children and I myself take the oath to be true and respect you people as our gods,

I'll take it first." He just leaned over in front of those two Kachina, and whack, whack right across his back, and his back just raised up with these welts.

It is so arranged that those being initiated into the One Horned Fraternity are always first. My godfather got right up and took me over there and stood up and turned me around and put my head right up against his stomach so only a little of my back was exposed. I was born chief and I must be respected. I kept my blanket on. I had a striped blanket. I had my blanket on, and I got one whack on the back, and my godfather just turned right around under those two Kachina, and he got the rest of it. Then we went back to the place where we were.

Some of those boys are supposed to know if they are either good or bad. They take his blankets up, and they usually just get one whack, and the godfather, he gets the rest. I was the youngest; I must have been about ten years old. The rest were from thirteen to fifteen years old. In those days they were not supposed to initiate anyone too young. They do the same thing with the girls. They take all the boys first, then the girls. They wear dresses. They are not supposed to be as bad as the boys.

When everything was over, the kiva chief says, "That's enough. You have done enough to us. I'll take your whips now." He laid them down beside the fire. Then he gave them a prayer plume. All during that he asked them to send rain so that the crops will be plenty and so that everybody will be prosperous.

The Mother Kachina had a tray of corn of all colors. She handed it to the chief and asked him to divide it among his people, that there should always be plenty of everything. So the man took the tray and laid it down on the floor. Then the Kachina went home.

After the Kachina went out, the man took the tray and passed it around, and everybody got a handful. There was all kinds of seeds on the tray: watermelon, pumpkin, and corn. After that was done, the old chief told us that what we have seen in the kiva we must

Secrets

Initiation

never tell any other children, that they must know nothing about it. What we have seen we must keep to ourselves. We all left the kiva and went back to our homes.

Then for the next three days I fasted. I was not allowed to have any salt or any meat of any kind, just plain food. I ate corn dumplings without any salt. Anyone that is being initiated is supposed to live on that for three days. On the fourth day, in the morning before the Bean Dance, you get your salt in beans, the green beans that are raised in the kiva.

That evening after I had my meal with salt, just as soon as the night falls, mother asked me to go ahead and sleep, and when the dance begins, my godfather would come and take me to the kiva for the Bean Dance until sunrise, and I must have sleep until the dance was to begin. When he came, he asked me to come along with him to the kiva. He stooped over and carried me on his back. Because I was young and it was dark, he carried me down to the kiva at Shipaulovi, and he put me down in there.

When I got in, I went to the right and sat down on a bench. The old man that was attending to the fire, he got up and picked up a tray of cornmeal, fine ground. The man drew a line with the cornmeal along the bench, up the wall over my head, and down the other side. That means I must not get over either line.

After a while the Kachina came. They were making all sorts of Kachina noises on the top of the kiva, and the man asked them to come in. The first one came in. I looked up. No masks; I recognize everyone of them! Of course I was then surprised that the men that I knew could make these sounds like the Kachina, and before that time I was afraid of the Kachina.

Then they follow in, in the same costume—just the costume for the Bean Dance. Then when everything is over, that is the time they tell you that you mustn't talk about it or tell anyone about it. If you do, a whole bunch of Kachina, more than you ever did see in your life, will come and put you to death with cholla cactus. Then they got you pretty well threatened. Then you just have to behave yourself. Of course, if you are mischievous, any kid will think about what he wants to do, but he never would talk about it.

It was two years later that I danced Kachina. The first mask that I got into was the Mudhead. I don't remember the year; I was just a kid. Anyway, it was a couple of years after we moved back to Shipaulovi, and that was the reason that they came after me. When we boys played Kachina, that took place in Mishongnovi, before our move.

After having the first time in the kiva, when they had these beans planted, the initiation took place four days before the Bean Dance. Then you go and see the Bean Dance for the first time. The children that are not initiated are not supposed to see the Bean Dance. The children are not supposed to see any dances done without masks. The Bean Dance is not masked. During the Bean Dance, the big ceremony when they have a big parade on the street, they take off their masks.

The Bean Dance will be the first time you learn that the Kachina were not really spirits but that they were being imitated. That was a surprise to me. I was the youngest to be initiated that year. After the dance is over, the kiva would precaution you not to tell any other children that have not yet been initiated. They say that all these things are only for you to know.

5

Life at Shipaulovi

We stayed on at Shipaulovi. Then after the Bean Dance we moved back into the Crane Clan house. There wasn't anyone living in the clan house. After driving us off, they were afraid to move in there. Of course, mother repaired the whole thing again.

In order to repair the clan house, it really needed new whitewashing and plastering. This is all that had to be done. The top roof was kind of worn, and we had to carry a lot of clay up there.

The house is in the old style of house. It was a three-story house. It has a porch on the first story, and the porch had a roof over it. And then there was another porch on the third floor. In the old Hopi house, the first floor doesn't have any door. There always was a hatchway down into the first floor, a ladder to the second floor, and either a ladder or steps to the third floor.

The house had three rooms on the first floor, all about ten feet by thirty feet, and the second floor had three rooms also. But, of course, on the second floor the rooms were quite small. The third floor had two rooms. There was a ladder up to the second floor and steps up to the third floor. They were along the side of the wall, and up to the roof there was another flight of steps. There was always steps up to the roof on any house. Any house that has a hatchway through the roof into the first floor is called a kiva. Or inside the room a hatchway down to the first floor, it is called a kiva, too. A kiva means where a ladder is leading down through the roof.

The back rooms on the second floor were laid out so that the corn could be stored there. There was a place on the third floor where the fraternity's ritual things would be kept. The place was just a little closet. It was just a small room about five feet by five feet, and the altar would be put there, piled up. It would be wrapped up in an old wedding robe, or it might be just an old cotton blanket, which was really made for that purpose. It would be just plain. Well, after we moved back, all these things were being kept there all this time. The uncles kept the Kachina masks there all the time, in the corn room.

One day I came home from someplace; anyway, I was out playing someplace and I came home, and nobody was home. First I look in all the rooms for mother, but she isn't home. As soon as I found out there was nobody there, I went up into that little room. It was way in the back, and I didn't have much light back in there because there were two other rooms in the front, and the porch. I looked up there and saw a mask hanging on the ceiling. I wanted to get my head in that mask to see how it would feel to have it in a mask. I wanted to pile something on the floor to stand on, but I couldn't find anything. I look around and pretty soon I see this pot, about two feet high, so I drag up this pot. I get on top of that, and I still had about two feet lacking. So I bring up a lot of bedding and roll it up and pile it criss-cross. In order to make it safe, I just open out a rabbitskin blanket and laid it on top. Then I got up there and got my head into the mask, but the eyes were just about even with my eyebrows, so I raised up on my toes.

All of a sudden the pot just went Pop! and down I went, holding on to the mask and my head still in it. The bedding was everywhere, and so was the pot. I jump right up and start putting the bedding back. I picked up the mask and threw it way back over the corn, and

I sure had to hurry to put the bedding back in the next room the way I found it. Then I went back in the room and picked up all the pieces of the pot and carried them out and threw them way below the mesa. After that I came back and got my bow and arrows and went out again.

When I came home that night, I made myself to not think anything was wrong. Mother didn't know until after a few days she missed the pot. She thought some other relative had come and borrowed the pot. She asked me, and I told her I don't know. Then again she noticed that the mask wasn't in its place, and she picked it up and noticed the string on the top was broken. The binding on the mask was broken, too. That's how she knew that somebody had been playing with it. She asked me if I had some other boys with me helping me get this mask down. I told her no. I told her I tried to get my head into it and fell down with it. She asked me how I happened to reach up there. I said, well, I piled a lot of bedding up there. But still I didn't tell her I broke the pot. I don't know what somebody was doing down below there, to bring up a piece of broken pot, and mother recognized the pot. Then I had to tell her I broke the pot, but since I was the only boy in the family, she would feel like she just can't punish me. So me being the only boy, everything was all right. She didn't tell the uncles.[24]

Then I was getting so I was pretty mischievous. I used to go out and shoot at the birds and shoot after the dogs. Now the Hopi believe that a dog will always revenge. They were always precautioning about meddling with the dogs, but of course, you know I always liked to shoot, because I was a pretty good shot with the arrows.

One day I came home with a rat I killed up in the rocks. I had a dog, and he was lying beside the door, so I thought it would be fun

24. Edmund told Whiting that Hopi parents were reluctant to punish a child, for that might cause the child to wish for his own death. An only child, in particular, was not usually punished. Any strong disciplinary measures were customarily administered by the mother's brother rather than the child's father.

An early photograph of Walpi, a typical mesa-top Hopi village. (Photograph by Putnam Studios, Los Angeles; courtesy of the Department of Archives and Manuscripts, Arizona State University Libraries)

Edmund and June Nequatewa in 1934. (Courtesy of the Museum of Northern Arizona, photo no. 9505)

A typical turn-of-the-century Hopi home at Mishongnovi. (Photograph by Underwood and Underwood, 1903; courtesy of the Department of Archives and Manuscripts, Arizona State University Libraries)

The trading post at Keam's Ranch in about 1890. (Photograph by Ben Wittick; courtesy of the Museum of New Mexico, neg. no. 16307)

to see if the dog would eat the rat. So I put the rat up by the dog, but he wouldn't take it in his mouth or even look at it. So I got mad and got a strap. This strap was about ten or fifteen inches long. We used to use them for ropes, for lariats. I was mad at the old dog because he didn't eat the rat.

Just then mother was going out after water. She came outside with this water jar. She had it wrapped up in her blanket. After their dresses are worn out they will put patches in it. She had her jar wrapped in this blanket, and so she left it on the ground in front of the door. She was going to bring some clay to patch up the roof, and she went up on the roof to see how much clay she would bring along.

So while she was up there I put the strap around the blanket and tied it. All this time I was calling to the dog and trying to get him to get up, but he wouldn't, so I put up my arrow and pulled the string and shot the dog in the ear. He just jumped up with my arrow in his ear and just yelped and ran. The jar rolled over and pulled the dog down the steps. It sounded like somebody dropped a bomb. Mother came running down and said, "Where is it? What popped?"

"Oh, the dog went around dragging your water jar."

I ran after the dog. He was still going, and all the rest of the dogs were after it. The other bunch of dogs were howling and yelping because my dog was. I shook the pieces of jug out of the blanket and took it home. My mother just had to get a new water jug.

Of course, she was mad, but she couldn't do anything to me. She realized I was the only one she has. If you have only one child and punish him and treat him mean, they are apt to get mad and condemn themselves and wish for their own death. So that is one thing they always have in mind, in any parent among the Hopi. For that reason she couldn't do anything to me.

So then my father insisted that he take me to the fields or go out herding sheep. So I go out with him, but sometimes if he wants to go away someplace where it would be too far for me to go with him, well, I just have to stay home.

It must have been after that, after we boys had been initiated, that a cousin and I went into the kiva and found a Mudhead mask. We turned it wrong side out and put it on. On us it looked like one of the most respected Gods, Masau'u.[25] We thought we might scare some of the boys in the kiva, so we went up to the village and gathered up a number of boys. We told them that down in the kiva we had found something awful funny. So we persuaded them to go down with us into the kiva. We had this old mask in the corner, right in back of the ladder, and while I was getting the boys down at the front of the kiva, my cousin was putting the mask on. I kept looking back to see if he was ready. When he was ready, I looked back and acted as if I was scared and started to run for the ladder. But before I could get to the ladder this devil had jumped on the ladder, so I ran back into the corner again. He started to chase us, and we started for the ladder again, but he was there before us. These boys were really scared, and of course I was pretending that I was crying my eyes out from fright. Finally I ran to this cousin and grabbed him around the waist and took his mask off. Then, of course, the boys saw that it was only my cousin that had the mask on. We had those boys scared up pretty bad that day!

It was in the spring of the year one time, and I was out shooting birds. I came home and I looked up at the house and I saw that all the doors were closed. There is always an opening above the door where anything that is being left over from the meal, like corn dumplings or a bowl of peaches, can be stored. When I looked up at the door, I find it was closed, but there is a bowl over the door. In

25. Masau'u is a Hopi deity concerned with death and is much feared. He sometimes appears as a masked figure in certain rituals.

that hole about one foot by two feet, there is a bowl up there. Our door used to have a crack right in the middle about an inch wide. I thought I would shoot my arrows through that crack into the house, on the third floor. I went up on the kiva roof and I started to shoot up there, about ten arrows. I would almost get the arrows in the crack. I had arrows sticking all over the door. So then at last I had only one arrow left. I wonder what is up there in that bowl. I wonder if I could break that bowl. I aim for that bowl. I just hit it right in the center, and it broke right in the middle and out came all that juice. It was a bowl of peaches. You should have seen that striped door! I picked all my arrows out of the door, and I didn't want to stay there. I got me one whole piki and went around the other side of the building, and there I was eating my lunch. I didn't want to take the bowl back.

I went over to Mishongnovi, started over there quite late, to see Vivian and the other aunt. I stayed over there quite late. They asked me if I wanted to sleep there. I told them no. Grandfather says, "You better stay, for it's quite late and pretty dark." I told them, "I'm not afraid of the dark. If I see anything in my way, I'll shoot them." They say, "We'll find out whether you get there or not. Don't cry on the way." So I started out.

I went down off into the gap. I went around on the right side of Mishongnovi. I was going along the trail. Of course, you know, I didn't want to notice anything. I was just looking one way. I had my eyes on the trail so I won't see anything. I was going along like that, and all of a sudden something spring right out from under my feet. I didn't do a darn thing. I just went over like that—easy. I don't know how long I laid there. After I came to, I remembered that Grandfather told me not to cry, so I didn't cry.

I walked on home, and when I got there mother was all alone, so I ask where my dad was.

"Your dad has gone out to look for you. He thought that you

might be over to Mishongnovi with your aunt. He must have gone on another trail."

"I came up on the east side."

"No wonder you didn't meet him on the way."

Afterwhile he came home and I tried to get to sleep, but I couldn't sleep. This thing that scared me—every time I remember I just jump up and make a great fuss. In the morning Father asked me what was wrong.

"What were you doing all day yesterday? Something must have scared you, because you were jumping up all night."

I told him, "Something scared me just before I came on top of this mesa. I don't know what it was."

My father said, "I know what it was, an old cottontail. That old cottontail scared me many times. There is a bunch of grass growing down there that comes up in the spring. This cottontail is always there when I come home at night."

So in order to prove whether Father was right, I come by there, and after I had seen that the cottontail was there, I wasn't afraid anymore.

The worst thing I ever did, it must be around about May. My father was planting a watermelon patch. It must be about a mile east of Shipaulovi, down in the valley. The wind was kind of blowing hard, and my father usually sent me over there every time when the wind blows so I can kind of keep the plants clear of sand so they won't smother. The wind was blowing good and hard, but it kind of calmed down in the afternoon. So I wanted to go over there in the afternoon so father wouldn't be getting me up early in the morning. He always sends me over there early in the morning, but I wanted to go over there in the afternoon. One thing: I always did carry my bow and arrows because I sure did love to see anything I could find to use for a target. I love to shoot at it.

I started down there. One of my aunts, she was just at the stage where she would wear her hair fixed up on the side of her head in a butterfly curl. Mother asked her to go with me so I won't be coming home late, so we could get through before it gets dark.

So we started out, and as we are going along the road, way down below I saw a dove in a peach tree. I said, "Hold on. There is a dove in that peach tree." She said, "Never mind the dove, we're in a hurry." I just put up my arrow and let it go. I shot the dove in the center and it fell off the tree, and I ran over and picked it up.

I don't know what happened, but I pulled too hard on my bow string and it got loose. I pulled the arrow out of the dove, and I want to fix my bow string. So I ask this girl to hold the dove. Well, she takes it so easy. You know how girls are. She was holding the dove so easy, and it wasn't killed, and so it flew away. I turned around and the dove was going up. I said, "What you let it go for?" She said, "Oh, it got away." I said, "If I can't shoot a dove, I'll shoot you." She screamed and ran. I was so mad I just put up my arrow and took a shot just as she turned around to look back. The arrow went right through her hair. I lost my arrow. She just screamed and cried and started running home. She came home with the arrow in her hair just to prove that I really did take a shot at her.

So I went on to the watermelon patch and worked until it gets dark. I started home. When I got home, grandfather, my mother's father, was at the house. He was sure mad, because it was his daughter. This grandfather was married again, so he wasn't living with us anymore. He was mad because his daughter got shot, but he didn't say anything. But after I had my supper he asked me what had happened, so I told him about the dove and how I got mad and she started running so I shot after her.

The old man says, "Boy, you know it is always dangerous to shoot at someone. You might shoot her in the back of the head, in the ear or her eyes. Bad boys like you, someone will wish some bad calamity on you, so you better watch out." I didn't say anything. Mother didn't say anything. Dad didn't say anything. After my grandfather went away, then my parents talked to me.

"Grandfather was really mad when he first came. He must forget he was a boy onetime himself. But from now on, don't shoot after anybody. That is wrong to shoot after a person. It is all right to shoot after birds and lizards. How would you feel to get shot?"

A few days later a lot of us boys went down into the valley to shoot birds, and about toward noon we started home. Instead of going up to the mesa, we went down on the east side of the gap between Mishongnovi and Shipaulovi to a big cave. We went down into it. There was a bunch from Mishongnovi and a bunch from Shipaulovi. So we thought we would play a game down there, and we made two piles of dirt for our targets. We were having a time down there playing a game to see who would win. Whatever arrows were not in use we stuck on top of the pile of dirt, sort of just to one side. We Shipaulovi boys won the game once, so we asked them for their arrows, but they won't give them to us. They promise to give them to us after the next game if they don't get even with us. So finally we win again, and everybody's arrow was sticking on top of this pile of dirt. So the first boy from our side went ahead and took a shot. This was all planned beforehand when we were running back and forth. We had planned that we would run away with their arrows. One of our best runners was going to take these arrows. We shot to the Mishongnovi side, and we all went back, and this boy ran and picked out all the arrows. Off he went, with us after him.

There was a big sand hill there, and we went crawling up there, with them right after us. We kept throwing handfuls of sand down on these other boys and got sand in their eyes. They couldn't help but stop. So we went on. Just as I was getting up to the rocks, I turn around to see if anyone was coming. Zip! An arrow just went right in my leg, and I just jerked the arrow out. Gosh I was mad. I had only two arrows with me, which were my best ones. I sat right there, and the blood was running down my leg. I was so mad I was determined I'm going to shoot this fellow back. I put my best arrow up, but then I decide to take the one that was in my leg and shoot it, and keep my good arrow.

Two fellows were watching me. I thought I would just let the arrow go, but just as it got there one fellow raised up and Bang! I got him right in the shoulder. Well, he just fell over like he was dead, just to make those people think he was dead. By this time there was quite a few people watching from the village. They see this boy was shot, and they tell that it's him, and they came running down. The uncle of this boy came running down, and of course he had heard that I had shot this boy.

When I got on top of the mesa, my great uncle, my mother's mother's brother, came down with his bow and arrows, and this other fellow's uncle, he had a club and said he was going to kill me. My great uncle says, "Hold on." I had the blood dripping down on my leg, and I told him that somebody shot me. So we had to have all those other boys come up, and everybody was holding on to this boy and he was making out like he was so hurt. They pull the arrow and everybody says it's his arrow. I had got the right one!

Well, this boy's uncle says he's going to kill me right then and there, so my uncle says, "If you're man enough, all right." He knows that he won't do it. He says, "Go ahead. I'm here to see you hit him. Don't forget, my arrow is right here. The minute you hit this boy, you'll get it." Finally the people began to gather and gather, and we had a big argument. One old man—he was a young man in that time—he came running down. He was another relative of this old man, and he just bawled this old fellow out, called him all kinds of names. He told him that he wouldn't be man enough to hit me, otherwise he is going to be killed himself. "You're going to be killed if you ever hit this boy," he told him. My great uncle says, "You give me that club and I'll beat you up with it. Any man that is crazy, who makes such a threat on a boy like this, needs to be beat."

They took me up home, and my mother picked up some of these corncobs and an old water jar. She opened up the top and put some live coals inside and then put the corncobs inside and made a lot of smoke. I had to hold the wound against the mouth of the water jar so the smoke will come out into the wound. They always put smoke in the wounds when people had bad wounds. I couldn't hardly stand it. The other two fellows had to hold me, because if they don't make me, it would get into blood poisoning. They just smoked it, and after that they didn't even put anything on it. The only thing they did, my father had carded some of the wool, and they had washed it and they put that on top of it, but that was all. It didn't even swell up. So anybody that catches a bad wound, they always smoke it up like that. It healed up pretty quick. They done the same thing to this other fellow.

Then ever since that we were great enemies. Just among the boys we used to put up a good battle.

This was in the summertime. It was before the Snake Dance. I and my cousin, we thought of this scheme. We would play ghost on people, on the boys and girls. After the Snake Dance there would be a sort of give-away-presents. The boys would run out with a basket or a watermelon or something like that. The girls have to run and fight the boys for these presents. If the boy is caught, he will hold the thing up as high as he could. The first girl who could take hold of it, they would get it. It was always like that after every Snake Dance, and after the Flute Dance.[26]

Snake Dance gets through about five o'clock. Then they may start dancing again that night. It goes on for four days. Usually they

26. These two dances alternate annually in each village. Hopi religious performances are conducted for the society as a whole and are performed by designated segments of the society in accordance with a fixed annual calendar. This provides for a series of major rituals and an opportunity, in certain seasons, for as many minor rites as the group may wish.

would start the presents in the morning. The children would come out to the mesa, each with their corn or whatever they have to run with. We knew that they always have these events in the plaza during the night. We thought that we would play ghost and scare the people up.

We found an old hat, a felt hat, very rare in those days. We cut the hat in half. Then we got to have some kind of paint on the masks that we made out of this old hat. So it was a black hat, and what it needs was white paint. We didn't know just what to put on it. Finally we got the idea. We picked up the droppings of the chicken. When a chicken eats a lot of starchy food, there is a lot of white in the droppings. We picked up these droppings and rub it on our hand, and it was kind of soft like talcum powder. We first experiment on our hands like that, and it stuck. Then we went around to all the chicken coops, looking for this white stuff. We get a lot and we went back to the house. We were working there. So we got way down in the back kiva. There was a little opening around here we had for lights. We put the strings on the side of the mask where we could tie it back. We made white circles around the eyes and the mouth and paint up its face with white lines. Every once in a while we would try it on to see how it looks. After we get it all painted, we got to have something for decoration on top the mask. First we thought that we would use some hair. That won't do. Then we thought we'll use some feathers, but how we going to get feathers? Then we thought we will use chicken feathers.

If we are going to use chicken feathers, we are going to use lots, so why not kill a rooster? One night after dark we went along where the chickens roost and we find some good-sized roosters. We walk up to them and they were sound asleep. We grab one by the feet and it just flap and squirm and kick and try to get away. Then we catch it around the neck. Then we get its feet to carry it by. It was then choked to death. We set our foot on its head and pull it off. We each killed us a rooster that way. Then we wrapped them up in our blankets and took them back into our kiva. When we got them out of the blankets, we had the blood all over the blankets. We thought, It can't be helped that they'll know we are the ones that did the murder. We don't have any lights, it was dark. We left our blankets there and we went on home.

Next morning, as soon as we eat breakfast, we pretend we are going out someplace to go shooting. We make everybody believe we are going someplace. We sneak into this place with our roosters. We start skinning the chickens. We each had one. We skin them and then we put the skin right on the back of the mask so the tail was right on top of the hat and the wings were over the ears. We realize that the skin would just dry out, so for reinforcement we found some old rags and sew them on for the back end of the mask. Then we stuck the skin on that part. Everything was prepared.

We got to have maiden shawls, too. Where are we going to get it? Finally we decided we just use an old ragged dress because grandmothers always have them lying around. So we went and stole somebody's grandmother's old dress. His grandmother was still alive. I got hers, but he got somebody else's.

Finally the set day came around, and all this time we have been going back there and trying these things on. We see that we look terrible. It happened, though, that when that day came there was a full moon. We knew that the plaza had people in it every night, but on account of the full moon we knew that if anyone happens to see us, and if they would have nerve enough to chase after us, we would have to jump over the bluff where there might be a cliff. Well, so we thought, What we going to do? Where shall we go? Shall we jump over the bluff or shall we run for the cliffs? So we just gave up. We didn't even come out. If we were caught, if the people didn't get scared, we would have to run for our lives. It would give us a bad reputation.

But there was our masks! Once or twice we went out in the moonlight to see what we look like. What are we going to do with these masks? We can't leave them in here. Someday one of the family will come in here and find these things. They will think that someone in that family is a witch that has been causing all these troubles. The next evening we had to take these masks and throw them away someplace.

We didn't do anything then until the next day. What we will do is to get some food as a ritual gift to this mask and take them away someplace and hide them. I went up around home and looked into the piki closet, and of course, you know, it was just after the dance, and mother had made a lot of piki, and there was still some fresh there. I got one whole one. I took it under my arm and went down there. After I got there and showed it to my cousin, how much I got, he went out to the place where they were staying and got his. We hid until the sun went down. So then we came out with our masks. We put the piki right inside of the masks and carry them out on the north side of Shipaulovi. Just as soon as we get down on the first ledge we went out west on the big ledge where there was a cliff. Before we throw them down, we take them in our left hands and swing them around our heads to "charm" them so nothing, no calamity, would befall us. Every day we will pretend that we are out shooting, and we would look down and keep seeing those things.

I have been telling you that my parents never would whip me. This is the first time my father ever did whip me. This was one time he came home on horseback and he must have rode the horse pretty hard. This was one of the new ones that he was breaking. He came home, and there was steps leading up to the third floor. The horse still had the rope, so my father, in order to hold the horse so it could not go away, he tied the rope around the steps, which usually they would stick out so much on each side. Anyway, I was playing on this porch. Mother was making piki. My father came home and went upstairs. I looked over the wall, over the steps, and there was the horse. He had his head down like this, sound asleep. I thought, That horse is sound asleep. I wonder what it will do. I think I will scare the horse just to see what it will do.

Mother had an old sheepskin in front of the piki stone where she rest her knees while making piki. I looked again and there was the horse. I got the sheepskin and got it out good and far to drop it on the top of the horse's head. Then I let it go. That old sheepskin landed right on top of the horse's head. The horse spooked and just rared right up and knocked out three steps, right out of the side of the wall. When that thing dropped, it made a loud noise. Then my father came running out. He started to come down the steps, but three were missing.

"What are you trying to do?" he says.

"I was trying to scare the horse."

"Well, you did it, all right."

He was sure mad. He picked me up and gave me a good whack right across the backbone three or four times. I was so scared I cried my eyes out. My mother looked over the steps because she can't get down. She had to take another ladder. She says that I deserve it. It was about time I got a whipping. She didn't even ask me to come up. That is all she told me.

I stayed there. I knew that place was good and warm. While she was making piki I got some and I wasn't hungry. I would just spend the night there. I went up to the piki stone and put my hand on it. Mother kept an old blanket over the piki stone to keep it clean. I had to put my hand on it to see if it was cool enough for me to lie down. It was, and I just lay down there and went to sleep.

Toward morning I felt cold. I put my hand under the piki stone, and it was just about right, so I crawled in there. The next morning my mother found me there fast asleep. She got me up, and one side was covered with ashes and one side with soot. I didn't see what was on my face. I went out, and my mother heated some water and gave me a bath. I thought, Well, I don't want to do anything. I don't want to go anywhere. I just want to pretend I am sick. So I went to bed and stayed there all day.

My father had to chase after the horse the next day. It was one of those broncos.

I didn't tell you the time we ate some jimsonweed. It was in the springtime, probably a little more toward summer. The jimson-weeds were in blossom, and I and two other boys had been out shooting after lizards and birds and many other things. We came up around on that table or bench, and as we were going along around the foot of the main mesa, we notice there is a lot of moths flying around. These gray moths, about two inches across, they look like hummingbirds. They would go into the blossom and go around like the hummingbirds would do. We saw them, so we went and picked one of those blossoms to see if that moth had really got something to eat out of there. We took the flower and tear it up. In the center of it, the pistil, we open that and there is sort of a watery substance in that. I took a taste first. It was sweet. And then I let the other fellows taste it. It was sure sweet. I took it away from them and ate it, and then that thing tasted so good that we just went around to see which one could get the most of it. If we would see a clump of it, we would just run for it. We went around, clear around the Shipaulovi town. After we got through, we went home. We got home just about when it was getting dark.

When I got home I didn't feel quite so hungry. I just had a little bite. Then I got so sleepy that I went to bed. Along about in the night I was dreaming. All of a sudden I must have jumped up and I don't know what I was saying. Anyway, I had the vision that there was a horse that came up on the porch and just climbed the ladder like a dog. And then it laid down on the porch and several other kids came up and they were all little girls. They jump on the horse and I jumped on the horse, and off it would go right over the ladder just so easy. Then we would all slide off. Then the horse would run around the kiva roof, and then it will start back again and just climb up the ladder and lay down, and then we will all follow and get on it, and then it will jump up again.

I began to feel that somebody was holding me down, and I was just kicking to beat the band. I began to notice the light, and there was my father and mother, trying to hold me down. I heard my dad say, "Sonny, where have you been all day?"

I looked up and say, "I have been out shooting birds."

"Are you sure that's all you did?"

"Yes, and I killed some lizards."

"What else?"

"We didn't kill anything more."

"At whose house were you before you came here?"

"I didn't go to anybody's house."

"You must have ate something someplace."

Finally I must have belched up, and he smelled of my breath. It was worse than whiskey. Then he didn't know what to do with me. He didn't know how much I ate. Finally somebody came in. They had called my grandfather, my mother's father. My parents were played out, so the old man came and he tried to hold me, and I just got right up and got out from under. After that somebody else came in. I just couldn't hardly see, but I just somewhat recognized the voices. One was my mother's uncle, who had helped us move back to Mishongnovi. He was the same man that was going back and forth all the time to get us.

"This is just what I thought. My boy is in the same condition." His boy was fourteen. "He has already thrown up. I have seen that these boys have eaten a lot of jimson blossoms."

Mother says, "What did you use to make him to vomit?"

"We gave him some stale urine."

So mother got busy and got some outside. In those days they save that stuff for indigo dye. My father was saving some, and she went out and got a dipperful. She put some hot water with it, and I didn't want to drink it. Finally they made me take it. I must have taken down only a mouthful or two, but just as soon as that stuff hit my belly, out she comes. Every time I get through, they give me another swallow. Then I start again. Finally I didn't throw up anymore. At least there isn't any to be seen. The old man was just crying. He thought that somebody had bewitched me. After throwing it all up, I went to sleep toward morning.

Just as soon as the daylight come, I was awake again. I got right up and went out to look for that horse, but there wasn't anything else but a dog out there. I was aching and sore all over. They had been sitting down on my arms and legs. They had been fighting me all night long. I was sore and blue. I ate some breakfast and went back to bed. I don't know how much I stayed in bed, but I was really sick after that.

This other fellow was really sick, too. After a few days I went around to see if he was all right. I went up to his house, and he was all right, but he hasn't been around. He was sore all over too.

The third boy, he didn't get sick, and afterwards we figured out what he did. He just took the blossoms up and smashed them in his hand and threw them away. He must have known about it. We are the only ones that got sick.

The old folks said that the spirits live in those plants. In fact, the spirits themselves are these little girls that live in these plants. The folks say that these little girls will make you a vampire, to play upon your opposite sex. They say that these little people would just work your mind and you will become half crazy or an idiot and that you would always be wanting to come in contact with the female sex. They will just make you crazy. The craziness would be relieved by sexual intercourse. They told us not to ever come near this place anymore, and they said that in case you happen to urinate anyplace, to look around and see if you see any of these plants, and if you do, get away because they are bad people. We had a good lecture on it.

From there on they got us so that we were so superstitious that every time we see that plant we will just run away. I got so that if I come near that plant, I sure can smell it. It smells somewhere between this four-o'clock and tobacco, only much stronger. Something like the blood after a woman gives birth. Sure is strong!

My grandfather recognized what the trouble was. He was superstitious. He thought that somebody made us eat the stuff. Grandfather says, "Somebody must have just bewitched these boys. Otherwise they never would have eaten that stuff."

This other man says, "I know who has been with them, but I have been to his house and he is not sick."

"He must be a witch, then, because if he did eat, and not being a witch, he would be sick, too. We can't do anything about it. If we do say anything, and if those people are witches, something else will happen serious. So just keep quiet."

I myself was just too young. I didn't think anything of it. This was before I myself was accused of being a witch.

6

More Moves Between Villages

This was in the springtime when the planting season was pretty well on. The people on Second Mesa were started going out into the fields to see how much readiness that they could make around there before putting in any crops.

The first crops that they would put in would be what they call the Kachina crop. The Kachina crop is a sweet corn or any corn that would bear or get ripe much earlier, like eighty-day or ninety-day corn. They will be rather light, sort of flint color—sweet corn. The yellow corn would be in the Kachina crop, too, and also the violet corn. The watermelons, or what are supposed to be the early-bearing watermelons, were at that time these red-seeded ones. After all the seeds for the early crop are being put in, then the bean planting season comes along. On the bean planting there usually were working parties—that is, the planting party. Several men—probably anywhere from fifteen to twenty-five men—would go out and plant for one man. These parties were going on here and there.

My grandfather, my father's father, he wanted to have a planting party, and of course my mother, being the daughter-in-law, had to furnish the food. Instead of going over to Mishongnovi, she started her fire under her piki stone quite early that morning. She was just about beginning to start her piki-making when one of these women that was always after her came up again.

She was about halfway up the ladder, and she said to my mother, "I thought you would be over in Mishongnovi by this time."

"No. I will not be going over until I get this piki, because over there the working party would be crowded, so I thought it best I would make my piki here and then take it over. But why do you ask?"

This other woman says, "Oh, nothing."

"But there must be something. Otherwise you won't be looking around here again."

"I came around to tell you that if you would start over there, that you must not come back again."

"Why do you say that I am not to come back anymore?"

"If you leave this house, then we can move in."

"Well, why had you not moved in when I left here before? Do you think that if you would be smart enough and had a lot of nerve, you would be living here now? Of course, you never do come around until you figure out all the lies you can pile up on me.[27] If you do feel that I should leave the house, that you should live in this house, it's all right with me. I never will be happy anyway for being in Shipaulovi." Then this other woman went away crying and my mother went on with the piki-making. When she used up all her dough, made it into piki, then I and her went and got ready and went over to Mishongnovi.[28]

When we got there, Grandfather was all ready to go out. He had three burros saddled up. One had a pack of lunches, and one had

27. Gossip as a form of social control is probably universal. In Hopi society it is a finely honed art about which much has been written. See, for example, Cox's essay "What is Hopi gossip about?"

28. The villages of Shipaulovi and Mishongnovi are only a few hundred yards apart.

two pottery water jugs, one on each side, and the third burro had a pack of seeds—beans. I was asked by my grandfather to ride the burro with the two water jugs, so I hurriedly ate my breakfast and got on the burro and started off with Grandfather. From there we started north along the bench. Then we went up to the spring. We filled our water jugs there. They had corncobs to cork them with. After the water jugs were put back on the burro, I got on again. From there I had to go very slow to guide the burro so I didn't bump the jars against the rocks. From there we went about a mile down off the mesa. You know where those two peaks are, northeast of Mishongnovi. We went around on the north side of them.

Shortly after we arrived there the men began to come around. Just as soon as enough men come around, we started to plant the beans on a slope of deep sand. I was planting, too, and of course I didn't know much about planting. Some places I just pile my seeds right on the dry sand, and by doing that I thought I would keep up with the rest of the men. Finally one of the men came over, thinking I would be doing just such a thing as that, since I was keeping up with the men. They knew that no boy could keep up with the men planting. He dug into a hill that I had been planting and he found that the beans were only an inch underground. Then they ask me to go back all over again and put them in deep enough, about two and a half inches down in the moist sand. Since some of these men made fun of me, I won't do it, so I just throw my stick down and walk back over to the place from where we started.

Just about this time a man came around with a band of sheep. Then Grandfather came running over and asked me to herd sheep so I won't have to plant any more beans, so that the man that was herding sheep would take my place. So I went on herding sheep for the rest of the time until the planting was finished.

A digging stick is about an inch in diameter and would be anywhere from three to four feet long. It would have a sharp, flat edge like a chisel. The proper way to use a digging stick is to kneel down with one leg and dig around on your right side. In the bean planting, you have to dig both sides because the beans would be planted about two feet apart. First you dig on your right side and put your seed in, and then turn around and dig on your left side so to be doing two rows at a time. For beans you will be making holes about two inches square. When you put your seeds in, they are not just piled in. They are laid separately so that they won't be touching each other, because if the beans would happen to be touching each other, they will decay and will not come up through the ground.

Then when the planting was done, the man came back over to the sheep, and I went back to my grandfather where he had the burros. He was ready for us to come home on them. I didn't want to ride the burro with the jars because I wanted to run home on the burro. I was just learning to ride then, and I like to see the burro run when I am riding. Of course, Grandfather was anxious to see me learn to ride, so he took the burro that was carrying the jars.

He put me on the burro and tied me on to the saddle because he knew I haven't been riding very much, and he didn't want me to slip off. When we started off, the first few trots I just hang on to the saddle horn. Finally I get brave enough so I took my hands off from the saddle horn. Then, of course, some of these men want to test me, so they just drive my burro along so I could go into a galloping just like the rest of them. That was some fun!

That planting party had their supper. The feast was given there at Grandfather's house. After supper my father asked Mother when we would start back for home.

"Don't you think we better start back home before it gets dark?"

Mother says, "No, we better not go back, so I am asking you to go up there after our bedding."

"Why?"

"Oh, we had a squabble again, and those women came around, and you know how they do. Oh, I think it's another time that we have to come back here. If we go back tonight, I know I cannot rest, and I am tired. Don't try to bring anything else but just the bedding, and then we will think it over, what might be the best thing to do."

My father went over there and got the bedding. Then from then on we were at Mishongnovi again.

All our planting was done from Grandfather's. What we did, we got all the seeds from Grandfather and planted for ourselves in our fields. My mother's fields were just left. The fields that my father was planting was the land that belongs to the One Horned chief, because they always had an allotment for the high priests. My father had his own land, but when he married my mother he had to use all the land that my clan had, and beside that he was planting this One Horned priest land.

Just before the main planting season was over, one of Mother's uncles, my grandmother's brother, came over from Shipaulovi. He asked my mother if we were not going to plant those fields. She told him no, to tell the other family to plant that field because if they want the house, they would also want that land. It was the One Horned priest land. My father was just planting his own land that year.

This man says that he will not do that, that he will plant it himself, that he may save the land from the weeds. My mother said, "Well, do as you like about it. It seems as though I don't have any support. I have no backing from my own people."

He knew that my mother was mad, and he didn't want to go any further into the argument, and he went back to Shipaulovi.

During that summer I remember well that we were in Mishong-novi, and everything went well until in the fall when these annual *wuwutcim* ceremonies begin. My mother's uncle came over again. When he did come, Mother didn't try to treat him badly; she was very kind to him. She offered him something to eat, as it is custom-ary among the Hopi that any caller at anybody's house should be offered at least bread or a drink of water—piki and water. Between meals, if a caller would happen to come, they will only be offered piki and water.

When he came to the door, my mother said, "Greetings. Over here. Be seated." She brought out a tray of piki, one of these yucca sifter baskets. The Havasupai baskets were used for meal. The coiled baskets that were in a bowl shape were used for water bowls to soak the piki to eat. They were black, decorated in white with simple designs. She set water in a bowl from the water storage, and piki from the piki closet, on the floor in front of him, and he is sitting on a sheepskin.

"Help yourself. Go ahead and eat."

After he finished eating, which was only a few bites, then he asked Mother to clear away her food. After she cleared everything away, she went back and sat down on the floor on a sheepskin. Then she asked him, "Why have you come again?"

The man says, "Yes, of course. I am sent over here by the members of the One Horned Fraternity. We are about to have a ceremony, and your boy being selected as a One Horned priest, we thought that it would be a good idea if you go back home to Shipaulovi and have a share of giving your food to the fraternity in the honor of your boy, which we thought would be the right thing to do."

"Well, then. All you men that are in that fraternity have well thought this out? If you did, and have decided to protect me and my boy from now on, I will go back. Otherwise, I will never return to that place. But I am telling you that I am not picking up my belongings right now and starting back. I want to hear from you men again before I make any move. You go back and ask them if they would be all willing to back us up and protect us. Of course, I know these ceremonies, as you all know, that it is these ceremonies by which all people live. Whoever goes back against their religion or any ceremonial rites will not exist. That is all. I am not going to say anything more. It is up to your people now to think this over."

Her uncle said all right, he would. "I think we are all willing to do what you ask of us, and I certainly will bring this matter before them tonight." He left and went back to Shipaulovi.

All this time the ceremony was getting very near. The next day the man was over again about the same time. He had news of what had happened the night before. Mother treats him again as usual with her food. After him getting through eating, Mother cleared away the food and went back and sat down again. Then she asked him if there was any decision made on her question.

The man says that every man in that fraternity is asking her to come back, that they are willing to back her up and protect her. But before she had given her complete consent, she told her uncle that she will move away again if another of the same trouble should come up. The man says that he don't think, or at least hope, that it will ever happen again. The man went back home to Shipaulovi.

Mother knew that what she had left at Shipaulovi must be all gone, so she asked Father to go out and get some wood and bring it to the Shipaulovi home. So then I and my mother get ready, and Mother got her cornmeal ready, and then we went over to Shipaulovi.

Father didn't have time enough then to go up to the cedars to get wood, so he went down to this old peach orchard, and what dead trees he found down there, he chopped them down and brought them up on his back.

When we got to Shipaulovi the house was in bad condition again. So, instead of making any piki that day, mother went to work and cleaned up the house, which took her all day. Then in the evening father went over to Mishongnovi and brought up our bedding.

That next day was a big day for the *wuwutcim* ceremony. Mother made piki all day. By evening she had a good stack of it, so when the dance was over, Mother took the piki to the One Horned Fraternity kiva in my honor. This made the men in that kiva very happy. From then on we would go to Mishongnovi once in a while and bring a few things up, because we had packed all our belongings over and had to carry them back again.

7

Experiencing Hopi Beliefs

The days and the months went by. The Bean Dance came around again. Just during this time my father and I went out after some wood, some of this greasewood, down to the wash with three burros. We loaded up the burros with wood and started back home. We were just about halfway and it started to rain. It was sure raining good and hard, and we were soaking wet, and some of those trails! On the burro trails Father had to push the burros. In those days the trails were so bad; they were more like climbing stairway steps.

Then, going up to Shipaulovi from the south side, my father had to push each burro, one by one, and left me below. Being an adobe hill, it was pretty slick. My father had to get the burros up first and then me. I was soaking wet and freezing, so I start crawling up on my hands and knees. Of course, I couldn't help but cry at the very top of my voice so somebody might hear me and help me up. Somebody certainly did hear me and came down after me, but instead of taking me home he took me into the kiva, and when I got in there they had a big fire. And just as soon as this man let me down on the floor they start taking off my clothes. What clothes I had on was a pair of pants my father made for me from overcoat sleeves; it was one of those army overcoats.

When I got warm in the kiva enough, I looked around. I saw by the fireplace there was a line of pots and bowls, with beans that were just sprouting up, about one-fourth inch above the dirt. I wondered what it all was. I must be pretty hungry, as I found somebody's leftover roasted corn and I picked it up and started chewing on it. By this time the men begin to laugh to think that I was so cold and hungry that I begin to chew on this corn. They were happy because I was saved.

Then someone says, "Well, somebody get the boy something to eat. Otherwise, he won't be chewing on that corn, if he wasn't hungry." It happened, though, from that kiva they were putting on a big ceremony. It was their turn which had come around to have this big ceremony, through to the Niman Kachina time. So the women are giving them food every evening.

Just then someone came and said to come out and take the food, and when they brought it in it was cooked beans. By that time I was warm enough and sure did feel hungry, and I had a supper to satisfy my appetite. After I pretty well come to, I was told that I was no more a child, that I am a man now, so that I must keep everything to myself, what I have seen in that kiva.

Just about dark my father came after me and took me home. From then on I had to go into the kiva every day. Now I was one of them, even though I was just a kid. But it made the other boys jealous and envious. I must have been about nine years old. As one of them, I had to keep on going to the kiva until the Bean Dance was over.

The night before the Bean Dance there is a Kachina that would come out and go around. Usually he comes into the village and runs and makes four rounds around the shrine in the plaza and then goes into all the kivas. This Kachina then runs down the trail out of the village, carrying away all the evil he has collected. Of course, the

Kachina spirit is supposed to grow wings and fly away. Actually, the man who plays this part will stop a little ways outside the village, where no one can see him, and take off his mask and ceremonial costume and clean himself up. There he will be met with his regular clothes by some member of the kiva group who is putting on this ceremony. Then these two people walk back into the village so that they will not attract attention.

Now this particular year, this Kachina came out of the One Horned Society kiva. Since I had been saved, or "captured," by that society, I had to keep going back there every night before the Bean Dance. That night, while the man who played the Kachina was out making his rounds, the men asked me to follow him off the mesa and take his blanket to him. I had no idea about how this was supposed to be done, and I was very anxious to do it just right. So I got everything they gave me folded up and ready, for he would come to our kiva last.

Finally he came in and made four rounds inside the kiva. This is the Kachina that is supposed to charm everyone in all the town of evil, and just before he jumps on the ladder, everybody would spit on him, which means that if you have any bad thoughts at heart, be sure and spit it out on this Kachina. It can't fail to happen, because just as soon as he himself makes the fourth round there is a man at the ladder waiting for him with a prayer plume, and he has to stop there. Just as soon as he stops, every man goes after him with a mouthful of spit.

After he got out, I got right up and put my head out of the kiva hatchway, and he was still going four times around the kiva hatchway. Just as soon as he leaves there he runs down off the village, and I run right behind him. Everybody was watching around the village, and there I was, following this Kachina. He went down off the bench and then off the bluff. I follow him down. They didn't tell me I was to go around the trail, that he was supposed to be a supernatural being and I wasn't supposed to follow him.

But just as soon as I jumped down where he had, I just threw his blanket down and climb back up and came back to the kiva. Then the men told me I shouldn't have done that. They started an argument.

"Why didn't you tell him what to do?"

"I supposed he would know."

"How do you suppose he would? He never done this before. Somebody of you fellows ought to have sense enough to go about it. All these children up on top watching and now here we are, just exposing ourselves."

"He should go around this other trail where nobody would see him, and give him the blanket."

After the Bean Dance was over, a few days after that, I was taken sick. Something had happened to my knee. This is the same knee that I have been shot in. Nobody seems to know what sort of a disease it is. My knee got to hurting so bad, and I just drawing my leg together to ease the pain about five or ten minutes. Then I had to go to bed. I just can't sleep.

Everybody thought that this calamity has befallen me because I followed this Kachina, that this sort of a trouble would be always caused by a Kachina.

I remember well that I just can't get to sleep. I cried all night and all day. My knee began to swell up. I don't remember how long—a week—and then it had formed an abscess like a boil, and it began to get soft. When it get soft, it didn't hurt so bad. I must have been sick for several weeks, and they didn't know what to do with me. Then everybody thought the end had come for me, that I wasn't going to survive.

Two medicine men came to our house. My grandfather is a Kachina chief and was at Shipaulovi. He thought that by giving me a sort of charm workover I would get well. That didn't have no effect. Every ceremony, before it is the time that everyone leaves the kiva, they always brought this charm treatment off with a song and sprinkle ashes over the buzzard feathers. To charm anyone, they would hold a feather in their left hand, and it would always be the left wing feather. They will have the ashes ready and hold the feather, and while they are singing they sprinkle the ashes from the hand out on the feather. The song ends four different times. Every time the song comes to an end, the men come over beside you and swing the feather out toward you and blow the ashes off toward the hatchway. Two different men did this to me, but that didn't have any effect on me.

Then finally they call another medicine man. This one was a witch doctor. He came in and threw the cover off my leg and looked at it, and he kind of looked me over and felt me over with his left hand. Then he says, "It's too bad. Something must be done. Otherwise this boy will never survive. Of course, I can't tell you offhand that somebody is bewitching you. If you really want to know and find out who is doing this against you, I will have to do a whole lot more than this. If you want me to, I will do it. But if not, you just have to take a chance in bringing this boy through."

Then my father and mother says, "We sure like to have you do what you can, and if you can see and detect a person who is really against us, and you have something which we may know, we sure would like to have you find out."

The medicine man says, "It is up to you. I can't do that for nothing. You have to sacrifice whatever you have."

My mother says, "All right, my son is worth more than what I may have. It might have some value, but I'd rather see my boy get well."

Then the medicine man says, "It will be the fourth night that I will be here to go through all this ceremony, and we will find out, or I will tell you, who the person is that is going hard against you." Then they set the date.

Then my father says, "Well, what I will do, I will give the medicine man a horse."

My mother says, "I will give him my dress and my wedding boots."

My grandfather, my mother's father, says, "I will give him my blanket."

My father says, "The thing to do would be to tell my father so that he would be there."

That night, when it did come around, just about dark the medicine man came. He had a bundle of his medicines and other things. What little light we have was just a little brush fire in the fireplace, and they pulled me up where the light was, and I was kind of half sitting up. The medicine man was talking away, and finally he says, "Don't anyone get scared. Let's all be brave and hold your nerves."

He reached into his pouch, and he took something out of there and put it in his mouth and chewed on it and swallowed it. Of course, what he had done was taken the medicine that would give him the vision. Then he spit on his hands and he just keep rubbing it like that. Then again he reached into his pouch, and I was watching and looking very closely. I saw that he took the crystal out of his pouch, and he held it up to the firelight between his fingers, vertically. He was holding the crystal up to the firelight, and once in a while he would hold it up toward me and then back to the fireplace. He kept doing that, and finally he says, "Here it is. Take a look. There is your enemy." My mother went over and took a look.

"I can't see anything."

"If you look carefully, you will see that person."

"I don't see it."

The medicine man gave the crystal to Father. Father said maybe he will see and recognize the person. He didn't see anyone.

The medicine man says, "Can't you see that woman in there? It is a woman."

Then I began to feel anxious and I wanted to see. The medicine man came closer and hold his crystal before my eyes, but I kept looking and I couldn't see anything. He was the only one seeing something in that crystal.

"It's over, but I don't see why you can't see this person and recognize her."

None of us could see. My grandfather, my father's father, came in and walked up to the light, and there was the medicine man with his crystal, and he took a look and he couldn't see anything.

After doing that, then the medicine man came over to me and put that crystal right on my knee and suck through that crystal. And it seems that something flick right back into his throat, and he almost get choked. Father hit him good and hard on the back, and he brought it out and showed it to us. It was something an inch long and white, and he says that thing was causing all that pain in my knee. We didn't know what it was. Then he came over to me and kind of lay back, and he lay on top of me and put that crystal where he thought my heart would be. And again he suck through the crystal and did the same thing. He suck something out, and it almost choke him. Then he ask me to raise up a bit and lean over. He put the crystal again right on top of my head. He suck, and again he got something on the top of my head. He says these things could get away, so he had them in his hand so they won't get away. So he was holding tight on to them. When he got through he went out, and my father went with him, and he bury them someplace and then came back.

When the medicine man came back, my grandfather says, "Since you have done all this, what wrong have you seen? What shall we do? We want to know why we should have a sick boy."

The medicine man says, "I have to tell you the truth. This boy was born a chief, and you being his parents, and he is given the house and, of course you have to be here. But now I have looked into this matter for you and have recognized the person that is bringing all this calamity on you. This person is cleared away now, and they will do nothing else. And they are here too, and listening in. They are always invisible. To be a witch, they can always transform themselves into some other animal, or they will be simply invisible, insects of some kind. It might be something so small you won't notice, or it might be invisible."

So grandfather, my father's father, says, "I would rather have the boy than to have the house, or see him become a chief of the One Horned Fraternity, because I realize that he is worth more than the house and all the things that he has to take care of. He will never become a chief of this fraternity. From now on he is mine. So regardless of all what I have to do, I am going to be here from now on to care for him, and if he gets well, nobody shall ever take him away from me. I will teach him and tell him of the course of life that I want him to take. I don't care what objections, but he will never become a chief of this One Horned Fraternity. Whoever wants that and whoever wants the house, let them have it."[29]

The medicine man says, "All right. If you think that is the right thing to do, you carry out just what you like to do with him. He is your grandson, and if you have any future plans for him, he is yours."

My grandfather said, "Yes, he is my son's son, but from now on he is my own. From now I am not going to call him Grandson; I am just going to call him Son."[30]

Mother and Dad just bursted into tears.

After everybody got quieted down, mother took out her wedding

29. Edmund's paternal grandfather's statements here are an early indication that he intends to influence Edmund away from his One Horned Fraternity responsibilities and birthright as chief.

30. Like many tribal groups around the world, Hopi is a matrilineal society, in which much authority resides with the wife and her close blood relatives. However, the touching scene that Edmund recounts here is authentic. In early Hopi society it was understood that an older man who was responsible for saving a boy's life earned the right to adopt that boy as his son regardless of his blood relationships.

boots and her dress, and her father got his blanket, and they handed it all to the medicine man. Father says, "Tomorrow I will get you the horse, and you will have the saddle and bridle and everything that goes with the horse."

It must be pretty late. Soon after the medicine man left the house, the cock begins to crow and it was toward morning. That I plainly heard, because we had some chickens and they roost on the porch.

After that time I must have gotten worse instead of getting any better. I didn't know that my uncle was putting on a special dance and that he had planned it after the Bean Dance. This was a Supai dance.

One morning I noticed somebody leaning over me. I opened my eyes and looked at him, and I couldn't recognize who it was. I noticed that he was crying, and he says, "Can't you open your eyes?" I looked up and I didn't say a word. I don't remember that I said anything.

He says, "Be mercy upon us, that you will be better by the time that the Kachina come. For my sake and for the Kachina, I do hope that you will be better, because you being sick and ill is breaking my heart, and it will not only be me with a broken heart if something worse should happen." While he was saying that I heard my mother crying. Then after a while the only thing I did see of him, he was going through the hatchway out of the room.

Then my mother says, "Son, won't you eat anything?"

"No."

"You must, because you are weak all the time, and there is nothing wrong with the food. If you could only eat, you will be getting better instead of getting worse."

"Mother, I can't eat anything; everything smells. Can't you ask father to go and get mutton? I am rather hungry for meat. I still have a sheep in the herd, so if you want me to get well, get the sheep of mine and butcher it. I want some meat."

"You are not going to leave me?"

"No."

Just about this time my father came in, and my mother told him I was hungry for meat.

"Well, all right. If he is hungry for meat, he might be getting better now, so I think the thing to do is to get him some meat. He might like to begin to feel that he would like to taste something different."

My father went out that morning, and toward evening he came home with the mutton. Mother just cut up the meat in small pieces and boiled it. Boy, that meat sure smelled so good! She must have had it boiling for about an hour, and when it was done she poured it out in the bowl. And piki sure tasted good in that! Ever since then I began to feel much better.

One day I notice they are preparing the Kachina feast, and mother was making piki. Away in the night, toward morning, my mother woke me up and said, "Listen, the Kachina have come and dance in the plaza." So I listened and heard them. Then they went away. That morning, shortly after sunrise, they came in town to dance, and then the dance begins for the day. They got through in the plaza, and mother had gone into the plaza to ask them to come out to the westside plaza to dance so I could hear them. She would talk to the man that leads them around with the sacred cornmeal. He belongs to the Kachina priests who are taking care of the Kachina.

"All right, we are asked to go into the next plaza and dance for the sick boy, so follow me." He started off and they follow him. He made a path of cornmeal. That song that they dance with, I never could forget the words in Supai. From then on I began to feel better.

By that time this abscess had broken, and a lot of pus came out of there. It broke sometime during the night, and they had to pile a lot of sand on my bed so the pus will drip on the sand. I didn't know the skin is so thin, and I would be forming nothing but pus.

In order to get all the pus out of it, my father went down to the ruins and brought home some good-sized pieces of black obsidian. They were kind of hammered and then washed, and they pick out the sharp ones, and slit the abscess on both sides of my knee. They held my leg up and rubbed it out. Then they called my grandfather, my father's father, and he came in and looked at it. He said, "I will get something to put into that sore." And he went out, and toward noon he came in with a bundle, and he opened it. He had brought in this prickly cactus from the ledge. He had the bristles burned off. He open this up and just cut the meat out inside and then cut it up in half-inch strips and put those pieces of cactus right in the opening or hole and on both sides of the cavity. He tied it up and left me that way.

From there on he kept doing that every day. Every morning he brought in new ones, and when he gets there and open up the sore and squeeze out those pieces of cactus, they just drip out a lot of pus. The pus will just soak into it. It didn't seem to take very long before that sore got healed up. It seems as though the cactus would just soak the pus out of that sore.

After I first got up, I still couldn't straighten my leg up and was limping and had to walk on the toes of that foot. After the sore was all healed up, then grandfather came each morning and rub the leg and try to get it straightened out. Even today my toes are bent up because I used to walk on my toes. I have got one short leg.

That was in the springtime, about planting season, when I began to walk on my toes. When my grandfather or father take me out, I would have to ride a burro. But I really don't remember just how it happened that my leg got straightened out. I think it just naturally straightened out, though, because I got so I just couldn't stand that massaging anymore, because every time grandfather rubs it, it kind of hurts. In order to get away from that, I would get up early in the morning and just walk off the mesa and wait down in the peach orchard until the sun get up good and high, and then I came home.

Anyway, I always had a burro to ride to the fields or to the sheep camp about five miles north, up in that valley northeast of Mishongnovi. Then I got so that I could stay at the sheep camp overnight and work. I could drive the sheep up to the spring, that spring that is called *Asaiva,* but we had to haul water for ourselves. My grandfather had to do all the water-carrying over there because I wasn't big enough or strong enough to carry a big water jar, or even to hang it on a burro.

My grandfather being a big Kachina chief, and a Kachina dance is coming on, he will just turn the sheep over to me, and I herd sheep for four or five days. And of course he kept telling me that someday, after he is no more, the sheep will be mine.

Then the fall came on, and when all this winter ceremonies would begin, the *wuwutcim.*[31] The wuwutcim men will go to their kivas as fraternity groups, and then in those kivas they will fast for four days. Then on the last day there will be a dance, and all the men of the wuwutcim kiva will paint themselves up and put on their costumes with sashes and women's bands and all the ornaments that they can get on themselves, jewelry and shell beads. They get all the shells from the Rio Grandes. They wear necklaces, earrings, and strings of turquoise. In those days there was hardly any silver. What bracelets or rings they might have are brass. They got them from the New Mexicos, the Navajos. We used to give them watermelons and peaches and fruit in exchange for jewelry.

This kind of dance, you don't wear a mask. They would wear all the Kachina costume but no mask. The children go look on because they are not considered as Kachina. They are just men dressed up in a costume to go to a dance, so it didn't apply to anybody but who you really were.

Then in about a month the Soyal ceremony would follow. That is

31. This male initiation rite has several forms, which are discussed in many of the Hopi cultural references listed in the bibliography. Once every four years, an elaborate form of this annual ritual provides for the advanced initiation of most of the young men in the village.

the time they make a lot of these prayer offerings which they would distribute among the people. The men would go to the kiva with the materials. The willow they would cut in the springtime, and peel the skin or bark off, and then put away to dry. And then at this time they take them to the kiva, with the feathers and also the cotton yarn. Then they kind of whittle them out into the form the way they want them, and after they do that, then they paint them up. Then they attach the feathers on them. Of course, there are many different forms of these prayer offerings, which I can't very well describe.

The first prayer plume, or *paho,* they will make will be for the sun. Those will be made before everything else. Then a man having a family will make the same kind for his wife and his mother, if he still has a mother. Then for the rest of the family he would make one for every member. First of all, he got to finish the pahos for his own family, and then the rest of the members of his relatives, which would be only on one stick. And for the children, they are usually on these shoots. Then if he has any livestock, he also will make pahos for them, and all the animals' pahos are painted white. For the people they are always painted with copper blue or green. He must finish them all before evening, in one day.

Then in the evening the women will bring them their food, a feast of mutton stew and piki. After they would eat, they stay up all night, and nobody goes to sleep. They would either sing or tell the stories or legends of the different happenings of years ago. I was not supposed to know anything about this until I was initiated.

One of these times in the kiva, we got so awful sleepy away in the night, and they wanted to sing some new songs that somebody might know. Someone said that singing a song will not very well wake everybody up. Someone suggested that some exciting story might make us all open our eyes. There was one old man there whom the men think might tell us a good story, but he rather kind of hesitated and said he didn't know any stories. But, of course, he did.

The story he told was the attack on two young men. It was in the olden days, and the attack was by some Navajos, about three miles south of Mishongnovi. He said that these two young men were out herding sheep, and in those days it was rather dangerous because they were always expecting the enemy to attack. Nobody would be off anywhere away from the town without his bow and arrows or a few throwing sticks—boomerangs. These two boys were not very far apart. They each had a herd. It was rather late in the afternoon when they saw a cloud of dust on the south side of the Polacca Wash. All at once they realized that the enemy was coming, but they cannot very well leave their sheep, so they ran their herds together and started on with them.

It happened, though, that there was some man about the same place, and instead of helping the boys, he ran home to call for help. He yelled all the way, so finally the people up on the village heard him, which was a signal that the enemy was coming. The Navajos finally came up on the boys and surrounded them. After they were surrounded they just had to let the sheep go. The enemy was surprised how the two young boys had put up a good fight. The men from the village were running down to meet the enemy, and before they got there one of the boys was shot and killed with a bow and arrow. This boy that was killed was an albino. The other boy ran into a neighboring wash and went along the wash. Every time the enemy would come up, he would be kind of protected, from the walls. The enemy was able to drive the sheep away and started driving them on while the rest of them were fighting the two boys. This was about a mile and a half from Mishongnovi village.

These other Hopi who were coming to the rescue didn't see the one boy in the wash. After they drove the enemy away and then followed them for the sheep, they forgot all about that boy. They caught up with the enemy just when they crossed the Polacca Wash, and from there they were shooting back and forth. Three Navajos were killed. Finally they took the sheep away from the Navajos, and the rest of them ran away.

The people in the village thought that both of the boys were killed. Then away in the night, before these men that had chased the enemy came home, they heard somebody yelling below the village. Once in a while it would cry and then yell. Then somebody went down and found this other boy crawling up the hill. They found that he was shot in the hip, so they helped him up. The first man that got to him claimed him to be his son if he ever would survive. He took him to his own house, and there he fasted with him for four days, eating only certain kinds of food, without salt. It was just the boy and this man, because it was customary for this man to adopt him, because he has survived a fight, just as though he got him out of the grave. After the four days he was given a head washing and a bath, and got a new name. They claim that on such occasions the other name was bad luck and should be killed.

The storyteller in the kiva see everybody was wide awake. This old man had been living at that time. Now he was real old and couldn't hardly get around. When he came to the point where the two boys saw the cloud of dust, they all began to sit up to hear what had happened.

It is then that winter came on, and my grandfather had to be in his wuwutcim kiva most of the time. I was then taking care of the sheep. During this time my grandfather could not very well bring me a supply of water and food, so my father was getting me some water and would bring me food like piki and dried peaches or parched corn or sometime this bread made from boiled corn. It is made out of rather coarse meal of any color of corn, put into boiling water, and let it boil for five or ten minutes and then stir it up until it stiffens up, and they will just test it out, and when it cools off it is like bread. You just take it off with your fingers.

It was during this winter that I was accused of being a witch. The people thought I was a witch because I was so young, and it was rather peculiar or strange that I wasn't afraid of anything. I wasn't afraid of the dark or ghosts or anything like that. It was because my grandfather used to tell me that there is no such thing as a ghost or anything like that. He was a bone setter who also administered medicine. He told me this as I was beginning to get well from this sickness that I had. He would come every morning and start rubbing my leg.

"Now, Son, there was no such thing as you being bewitched to have this trouble, because I know. Whatever I am going to tell you, it is going to be the truth, because I want you and need you myself, and I am going to direct you into a different light of life. There is two different kinds of life in this world: darkness and light. The people that lead themselves into the darkness are the ones that are superstitious. They are the ones that are telling you that there is a witch or a ghost. There is no such thing. Now take this medicine man, this witch doctor. He will tell you that a porcupine quill has been shot into your heart or some other part of your body, which might cause you great trouble or even death. Now, there is no such thing. Any time you are sick, it will be because you are mad at yourself and wish for your own death. Anybody who claims to be a witch always carries one or two straws from a hairbrush. Don't ever let yourself believe that you can see things in the dark. Anything that scares you in the dark is your own imagination."

I don't know how many times he told me this, but he retold it to me many times in the mornings or when we were out herding sheep in the fields someplace. At noontime we would rest under a brush and eat our lunch, and there he taught me to say a little prayer before I touched any food: "May this food that I eat make me grow big and strong. May the mercy be upon me that I may have many days to live and will see things that will come to pass." This prayer he taught me that I might always say it in my own heart. I have done that to this day. He told me that he had learned to say this prayer from his own grandmother. She had taught him to go out at dawn with the sacred cornmeal to ask the rising sun to hurry the great Bahana[32] along so he might meet him face-to-face during his lifetime.

I was often left alone at the sheep camp, for my father went home every night. People wondered whether my parents or even my grandfather had any heart for me, to leave me out alone at the sheep camp.

One day it happened to cloud up and snow some, but very little, only an inch or two. When my grandfather woke up and found that it had snowed, he got up early and started out with his straps and axe and also some lunch. I was surprised to see him coming, and when he got there I asked him why he came so early. He said that he was afraid that I might be out of wood. I said that I was. So he went up on the hill to get some wood. He ask me if I might be needing some meat, and I told him yes. He jumped into the corral and caught a young goat and butchered it. He gave me all the meat and took home all the insides and the head. Before he left, he said he was going back up on the hill so he could get some wood and carry it home.

I was just letting the sheep out of the corral when my father came and asked me where my grandfather went. I told him he went up on the hill. I asked him why he had come. He said that somebody says at the village that the track of some kind of cat was seen going from our house and off on the trail down to the bench, but it was found that somebody came by in the snow and it seemed as though to cover the track he just walked along wherever the cat tracks were. He said that the story was told that the track of a cat is my track, so this man that came by early in the morning is trying to protect me.

---

32. At least some Hopi still use this controversial term to mean all white Americans, and some use it to refer to the white man's Messiah.

Wherever he had seen the track, there is where he would step. Father wanted to ask my grandfather if he had seen any tracks of a cat leading to the sheep camp, so he didn't stop very long. He went on up, following Grandfather, and I went on herding the sheep.

That same night my grandfather came back again to the sheep camp. There again that night he was telling me not to worry about that, because it was just a made-up story. That same night he told me that it will not be very long before I will be going to school and will learn to read and write and also to speak the *bahana* language. During this time one of his daughters was already going to school, and that fall he had taken his son into Keams Canyon. The next morning he went up on the hill and got a load of wood for me so that I was very well supplied with fuel.

With the sheep I had three good-sized sheepdogs. They were well trained and were surely a great help. Every day I would have a cottontail. These dogs would always catch one or two cottontails. And being a Hopi boy, I would always have a great heart for Mother; I would be saving these cottontails for Mother. I would roast them and put them aside up on the shelf, and when my father comes I sent them home to Mother. I laid them on the live coals, or to have them roast slowly, I just set one in front of the fireplace. I would dress them and save the skins.

In order to take the skin off a rabbit, you split it at the hind legs and front legs and slip it off. Then you have the case of the rabbit, and you would use it for an extra pair of socks with the fur inside. If there wasn't any snow on the ground and your moccasins don't get wet—and the skin get wet to your feet—it will last a long time. But if you get your feet wet, you come home sometimes and you can't help but tear it off.

What I would use is a goatskin boot. My grandfather used to make them for me all the time. These boots were sewn with yucca cord. This is simple to make. You take yucca leaves and work at it, maybe even chewing it, until the flesh is removed from the fibers.

Then you double it to form two sets of fibers, which are pressed against the knee with the heel of the right hand. When the hand is moved forward along the knee, the fibers are twisted together, and then if you release the right hand, these spun strings twist against each other to form a two-ply cord. Then you pick up the end of the last spun fibers with the left hand and continue the process with the rest of the unspun fibers.

The family that thought I really was a witch is still alive, and the woman of that same family told the same story at Grand Canyon when I was there many years later. This woman asked me about it and I said, "Sure I'm one of them. If I was really a witch I wouldn't be here. If I was really one I would be a millionaire right now!"

8

At Keams Canyon School

When spring came on, all the men were busy in the fields, and my father and grandfather have to do their planting, too. Most of the time I was herding sheep. Grandfather thought it would be best to move the sheep out near the fields where I won't have to go so far. The first thing in the morning, I would drive the sheep to water. As the hot days were on, there was sort of a water shortage, so we would drive the sheep down to the Toreva school, where there was the only big spring, where all the livestock used to water.

One day while I was out herding sheep, the wind came up and was sure blowing hard. Every once in a while I would lay down to rest my eyes because the wind was blowing so hard. There was not much space around the fields to herd sheep, and I had to follow them all the time to keep them out of the fields. But the wind was sure bad, so I kind of laid down, putting my head under a big bush with my blanket over my head. Once in a while I would look up to see if the sheep were still there.

The first thing I knew, I had gone to sleep and forgot about the sheep, and the whole flock went right through the field and just ate the corn clear down to the ground. It happened that just about that time my grandfather came along. He knew that the sheep should not be on the other side of the field. This was about two miles south of the Mishongnovi village. It was on a sand dune. You have probably noticed that white spot south of Mishongnovi, which is alkali. That is where all the fields were at that time. The fields would stretch up along the sand dune.

Anyway, seeing the sheep on the other side of the field, my grandfather has to run the whole flock right back through. The sheep will not pick up anything more on their way. After getting them back on the other side, he yelled and yelled. Finally I heard someone yelling. I jumped up and all my sheep were there, and I thought they never had been anyplace. My grandfather saw me, and he came running over. When he got to me he says, "Son, did you have a nice nap?"

"I don't know. I don't think I have gone to sleep. The sheep were still there when I raised up."

"I drove back the sheep. They were away on the other side of somebody else's fields. It is your hard luck. You have to give up one of your sheep."

I had about twenty in the flock that were my own. I looked at him and spoke to him in a half-crying voice, "Do I have to give up my sheep?"

"No use to cry. You are guilty."

"Do I have to give up my own sheep?"

"Certainly you have to."

"Why can't I give my daddy's sheep?"

"You can't do that. He is not guilty. You are the guilty one."

"Which one shall I give up?"

"You know your own sheep. So whichever one you think you want to give up, that is your business."

Then it was about very much toward evening, so I started to drive the sheep toward home. Then, getting them into the corral that evening, I thought I would look them over. And while I was in the corral, my father happened to come around. The corral was up toward the mesa at Mishongnovi, but it was down below the hills, beyond the mesa. It was a loose rock corral. Father says, "Well, is one of the sheep missing? Or why are you looking them over?"

"There might be one missing tomorrow."

"Why?"

"I went to sleep when I was herding, and the sheep got into a man's field and ate up his corn."

Father says, "I don't believe you better give one of the sheep."

"Why?"

"Because I want you to have your sheep increase."

"Grandfather says I have to give my own sheep."

"Well, never mind. I have an old ewe that we can let the man have." That was because my father realized that I have been working for him all this time, and for Grandfather. But I know Grandfather just wanted to teach me a lesson. That is why he says I have to give up one of my own sheep.

So after we found the old ewe, we tied a string around its neck. Then we close up the corral and went home. Just as soon as we got to the village I went straight to the man and told him what had happened, that my sheep had gone through his field and had done bad damage to his corn, and that I was ready to give him a sheep if he would come down to the corral in the morning. He was very nice about it. He didn't even scold me and said that he will be down to the corral in the morning.

The next morning early I went down to the corral. Then after a while he came along and we jumped in and I showed him the ewe. He caught her and tied her up. Then he put his strap around the old sheep and carried it up to the mesa on his back. The tumpline would pass between the forelegs and is doubled on both ends. In order to carry a sheep, the wide part is across the shoulder. All four legs are tied together. Carrying a sheep is worse than carrying a bag of sand. After he got home with it, he just cut her throat.

Anyway, I had the old man well satisfied with the sheep. From there on I never would want to lay down when I am herding sheep, no matter how hard the wind might be blowing, because I don't want to lose any of the sheep.

During that summer when the crops were pretty well along and things began to get ripe, like corn and melons, Grandfather's son, named Kachina, came home from school in Keams Canyon. We were out together every day, Kachina and I. By that time most of the busy days were over for the men, and my father would herd sheep, and so would Grandfather, and then it was our time to look after the fields so nothing would come and hurt them, things such as crows or prairie dogs. My grandfather was asking his son about what he had learned in school.

"Son, if you had learned anything, I think it will be sort of nice if you could teach your nephew a few words or talk to him in bahana, because when the time comes for you to go back to school, both of you will go."

Hearing that, I thought it would be great fun to go away with my uncle, and I would always be looking forward to that day when we will leave home for school.

It seemed like it was a long time before the day had come. One morning when I was not expecting it, Grandfather came up to the house. I was still in bed when he came in. He woke me up. After he got me up he said that we are going to Keams Canyon. I would be going to school with my uncle now. My father and mother had nothing to say, because they remembered that my grandfather has put a claim on me while I was very sick. Since then, my parents had consented that I would be his. Therefore, my parents didn't have a word to say, even though I rightly belonged to them.

After breakfast my mother packed up a lunch for me to take along, and father had put two melons in a bag. Then my father went to the corral and got the burros out and put the saddle on. I was very happy to go, so I got on the burro and off we went, I and my grandfather, and we went over to Mishongnovi. When we got to Mishongnovi, everything was ready. The burros had been saddled up long ago. Just before we left the village I thought of my bow and arrows, which I know that I don't want to leave behind. My grandfather went back after it for me because he could run up there faster. I couldn't run. When he came back with my bow and arrows, we started out, climbing down off the mesa on the east side.

I had been to Keams Canyon twice before. The first time I ever went to Keams Canyon was when they were issuing hoes, files, and axes and things like that. I have a faint memory of being there with my mother and her grandfather. Then the second time I went there it was during that same summer that I went to school, and they were working on a building at that time, a two-story building. Right in the center of the wall they had a date written, 1895, and that was not finished yet when I was there during that summer. Therefore, I really knew where I was going.[33]

After getting off the mesa we went on, it seems as though a long day's trip. We didn't trot the burros, and grandfather walked behind, driving the burros. We had three burros, but grandfather didn't like to ride. If he got tired, he got on and rode, though. Anyway, it seems it was many miles. Just before we got up to the school there are a lot of boys who were already there and came to meet us. They got on our burros behind us so that we all rode in up to the school.

That evening we went to supper with the rest of the boys, and grandfather went with us. After getting into the dining room, I was the whole show. Everybody had their eyes on me because I had long hair tied up on the back, with bangs, like the Hotevilla custom is now. I had quite a bunch of hair. It seems like that I had strange food for supper, not being used to the light bread instead of corn bread. I never had drank tea before. The worst of it was that they had poured

33. Edmund was sent to the distant Keams Canyon School. The first day school on Second Mesa would not be established until 1897.

some milk or cream into my tea, and I hated to drink it because it was warm. I never had drank anything warm before. All the supper didn't taste very good to me, and what I had took down all wanted to come up. It happened, though, that my grandfather got up from the table and started out, and I got up and started out with him. Just as soon as I got out of the door I let everything go. It was a relief to throw everything up.

Then I went on with my grandfather to the foot of the bluff, where we had unsaddled our burros. I asked Grandfather if I could eat something that I like. Then we cut up a watermelon and ate that with piki. While I was eating, Grandfather said, "Son, you have to learn to eat this food here, so whatever you do you just want to eat just a little at a time. Then you will certainly learn to like it. Because the reasons I brought you here—that I wish—at least I want you to—that someday you will have, or will be able to have, the quality of food that these white people will produce. And not only that, but that the time will come when you might be able to wear good clothes and wear out at least a few good things these people will produce. I doubt very much that I ever will be able to ride in the kind of a wagon that in the future may be invented. Remember that you want to look forward to that day. It is time now that you better make up your mind that you're going to stick to the school and learn all you can, which is my desire for you to do. I can never figure out what will come to pass, which I know very well I may not be able to see. I am afraid that I am getting too old. Though I do wish all these things that I have been telling you—and that I have been told many years ago—would come to pass while I am still alive. I envy you here. You just happen to be in the time that this school is started up. Many times I wish I was as young as you are, that I would be able to go to school. But I guess the man is only born once."

I thought then that it was the last night that Grandfather would spend with us, so we stayed with him for a while. Then somebody came along, one of the school boys, and said that it was time for us to go to bed, so we had to go to the school building. When we got into the dormitory, I looked around and saw some strange-looking things. I didn't know what they were, but Kachina told me that they were the beds on which we have to sleep. Then we both got in the same bed, and I don't see how I can rest in that bed. It was moving all the time up and down. Too springy! They were kind of corrugated iron affairs. They don't have any support under them, and when you lay down they just sank down. And if one person is heavier than you are, then just lie on one side. Every time Kachina would move he would wake me up. I could hardly sleep. Then finally I got so tired I fell asleep. I guess I forgot where I was, and I must have tried to stretch myself out, without remembering where I was. First thing I know, Bump! down I was on the floor. I got right up and crawled back on the bed. Then I just can't go back to sleep again for fear I might fall off again.

Early the next morning I heard a big bell ringing, one of those great big huge bells, and everybody got up and went to the end waiting room where there were many, many washbasins hanging up inside of the house. There was only three towels on a roller, on which everybody wiped their hands and faces. After washing ourselves we went to breakfast, and before we went in I was telling Kachina that I don't want to have that food again. He says we were not going to have tea that morning, but we are going to have coffee.

"What is coffee?"

"It is going to be black water. It's all right when you put sugar and milk in it."

"Anything like that I don't want to drink. If I am going to drink anything, it will be water."

"If you want to drink water, tell the waiter what you want."

When we got in, everybody stood at the table behind their chairs. On the first bell everybody bowed their heads, and I don't know what they said. It must be the grace that they had repeated. Everybody said it.

When we sat down to eat, everything that was on the table don't look like food to me, because it wasn't the corn dumplings. We had oatmeal, coffee, bread, and fried potatoes. Some of those boys, or the children, if they don't think their oatmeal is sweet enough, they would pour syrup into it, which was the awfullest looking mess that I ever saw, which I certainly didn't want to eat. Nothing tasted good to me, but if I want to be able to go to school, I have to eat it.

After breakfast my grandfather met me outside the door and said we have to go up and see the big chief, the big bahana.

When we got to the office where the superintendent was, my grandfather introduced me to this white man, telling him that I was his son and that I must be well taken care of. At that time my grandfather had been appointed a government judge, and he was well respected. The agent had consented that I must be well taken care of. He gave my grandfather a note, and he took me back down to the children's building to look up another white man, and when we found him Grandfather gave him the note. The man looked the note over and went inside the house and came out with a pair of scissors, and I remember a pair of clippers, too. He sat me on a chair and he went to work and cut my hair off, just like taking my scalp. Took it all off, down to the skin! He showed me a pile of hair, which had been on my head. I felt very light after that.

Then Kachina and I went to work and built a fire under the big cauldron and filled it with water. Just as soon as it got hot enough, they gave us a big tub and we went into rooms and filled the tubs up half full of water. Instead of having any toilet soap, they gave us this hard brown laundry soap to bathe with. Before we went in to take a bath, we were given a new outfit of clothes, shoes and socks, and a hat. After that bath we put on our new clothes. All that I had was one of these unbleached muslin shirts and the same kind of trousers, split up the sides, and moccasins and socks. The pants were white, more or less. The homemade trousers had a string on the top like a pair of pajamas now, and we wore our shirts on the outside like a Chinaman. I didn't have much to send back with my grand-father, just my shirt and trousers and moccasins. Kachina had on an old set of school clothes, and they gave him a new pair of shoes and a new set of clothes.

That was a long day. And there I was in the canyon and couldn't see out in the country, only the sky to look up at and the canyon walls on each side. Then I wondered to myself how long it will be before I ever see my parents again. I began to feel homesick before the day was over. The next day I went to school with the rest of the children. I was so homesick that I don't remember anything that happened that day.

The mealtimes I couldn't eat anything, and Kachina tried to cheer me up, but every time he talked to me the tears would be running out of my eyes. I wanted to cry, but I thought that I was big enough and ought to be brave, so I would only shed a lot of tears but would never let the sound out.

I was so homesick that Kachina went to the superintendent and told him how bad I was feeling. So he was given permission to keep me out of school, that we would just play around and go up on the hills and rabbit hunt and do whatever we wanted so that I may soon forget all about the homesickness. I thought to myself that I was very childish and foolish to be homesick, and after a week's time I was about as mischievous as the rest of the boys. All my homesick-ness had disappeared.

After going to school for a few months, every time when the mealtime comes I remember marching into the dining room and looking on the wall where the date was written, wondering what that meant. After I learned to read the figures, it was 1895, the year I entered the Keams Canyon School. About once in every month my grandfather would come to see me.

It was altogether a Hopi school, but there were boys from all the Hopi villages. The school at that time was more prejudiced because they locked us up each night. This was a big dormitory, and all the windows had bars on them. The bigger boys that had gotten sick just like I had, they had run off from there. It was for that reason that the dormitories were always locked every night.

No toilet facilities were provided. During the day we would look around on the floor, which was just built out of one-by-twelve boards. It was poor lumber with lots of knots. Those that can't get up to the windows to urinate crawl around the floor at night and urinate through these holes. Only the girls' dormitory was two stories, with the dining hall under the dormitory.

It wasn't very long before the warm weather comes around, and the whole place just stunk. Later on, these larger boys couldn't stand it any longer, because if we did get enough to eat, a person wants to get out during the night to go to the toilet. So it was quite a number of good-sized boys—practically young men—that decided that they will just crap all over the floor, which they did. The boys' advisor, or disciplinarian, or whatever you call him, . . . every morning after breakfast we go in the dormitory to do our work. This disciplinarian would give us the command to make our beds, like they would do in the military camps. He looked around and saw all this mess. Without having us make beds, we were all called out outside to form a line out there.

"Now, boys, whoever made that mess in the dormitory will please step forward."

All these big husky boys stepped forward. The disciplinarian felt pretty small to see those big boys in front of him. He asked them why they had done that. So the boys say, well, they had done it because they locked them up every night. So they either go without their supper every night or every morning they will find that mess there. "If you don't like that mess, take the padlock off the door."

"I can't take the padlock off the door because you boys get out and run away."

"All right, you keep the padlock on the door. And unless we go without our supper, you will find the mess every morning. If the superintendent told you to keep the padlock on the door, you go tell the superintendent to look at the mess. Show him the mess we made and see what he thinks about it. And if he doesn't like it, we will go home. We don't want to stay here."

I guess they did discuss the matter with the superintendent, but he couldn't very well take the padlocks off the door, so he gave us buckets every night.

It is natural for all the creatures of all kinds to fall in love, and the boys were then so well acquainted with the girls. Naturally they had their sweethearts, and it was customary among the Hopi that the boys would call on their girls at night. I was too young to know what was going on. Later some of the small boys found that these boys had been getting out every night through the bars on the windows. Before long, the pipes on the windows were in a bow shape where the boys helped each other. Two on each side would pull on the bars while two get out, and those two would then pull on the bars from the outside to let the rest of them out. These things must have always been planned ahead, because when they got around to the girls dormitory, the girls had hung down their sheets to pull up the boys. I don't know how long this had been going on. The boys would talk about the sort of fun they have been having. In those days it was nothing like today in these modern times.

The girls were very shy, and it was customary that the Hopi girl would not openly talk to her boyfriends in front of anyone else or before the public. Every day at mealtimes it was funny to see those girls eating their food with napkins in front of their mouths and taking pieces of food under these napkins to their mouths. You could only see their eyes rolling around back and forth. Some of us would make fun of them. We would pick up a napkin and tie it back of our head and reach out and take food in behind the napkin, just to make fun of them.

Seeing the girls like that looks awful funny. One day some of us got hold of rubber bands. We started shooting little paper wads, and then we would put the rubber band right down so they don't know who did it. Some of those girls just can't get enough to eat. If any of those girls have a relative, they always get them to pack out bread for them.

They were so bashful. The only relative I had there was the albino girl from Shipaulovi. She was not like the rest of the girls. Being albino, nobody paid any attention to her. It happened, though, that I made a friend with one of the girls from Oraibi. She would always ask me to pack out bread for her, because she was quite a young lady and I was only a little kid. I was doing that for a long while. She told me one time that she would eat better if she had syrup, and she gave me a small baking powder can. What I used to do, I would pick a pitcher of syrup and pour it in there, and carry it out like that, with a slice of bread. One day I did that again. We used to run out like a bunch of sheep, out through the door, just to get out. This time somebody pressed me right against the side of the door. I ran around to the side of the dining hall where this girl was, reached into my pocket, and what do you suppose I found? The can had been crushed and spilled all the syrup into my pocket. My hand came out with my fingers stuck together. I didn't lose any time. I ran to the spring and turned my pocket wrong side out and started washing.

Grandfather made his first trip back to Keams Canyon two months after he had left me there. I was sure glad to see him even though I had gotten over my homesickness. But when I saw him I wanted to cry. He knew that I was homesick, and he just kind of cheered me up. So I was all right, but I was feeling a big lump in my throat all the time he was talking to me.

I thought that he had rode a burro in, but I found out that he had walked in. He had his blanket on. The way he had the blanket around him, it was drawn up so there was room enough around back of his blanket to put all his stuff in, like a sack. He had quite a bit of room there, where he had put all this stuff. The blanket was a Hopi striped blanket. It was indigo color with black and white stripes. There would be one white stripe about six or eight inches wide and then a stripe the same size which alternated black and white vertical threads.

"Son, I have brought you some lunches—parched corn and piki that Mother sent. She thought you might be hungry for those things, because I did know that the first meal you had here didn't stay down very long."

I took the sack of parched corn and piki, but I didn't know where to put it, so I went to the dormitory and stuck it under my mattress. After I put that away I went and looked up Kachina. After finding him, I brought him to Grandfather. Just about that time the bell rang; it was suppertime. All the boys lined up, and at the command of the disciplinarian we all marched into the dining room. Grandfather followed us in.

In those days they used to feed any of the Hopis that were employed by the government. Every village had their respective representative, called judges at that time. They would meet there with the agent every two or three months to discuss with the school how it should be run. They didn't deal with any other problems. They thought that a limited number of years was enough for any child to attend school. Most of the children were sent there for four years, because most of them thought that four years was the limit. The judges, when school begins, they would go into the Agency and discuss the kids and find out whose time would be up. And if a student should happen to have an uncle or a brother or sister which they might send to school in place of the child that is getting out, that is the way they were working it. Somebody got to replace a graduate.

How much a child will learn depends on how much they want to learn in four years. On the average they will reach the third grade. They hardly learn to speak English. They really didn't have any rule about the language you spoke while you were in there going to school. Everybody spoke Hopi on the grounds, and the teachers all spoke English. The students would be able to speak some English, but they won't be able to speak enough to understand much of anything. I could understand all right when I got through with four years, but to get into a conversation, . . . just can't do it. You might be able to answer somebody's questions.

They didn't have any shops. They had an industrial teacher. All the boys would be chopping wood or tending their gardens.

The only thing they were learning in the classes was reading and arithmetic. I could read all right, but many times I really won't understand what I was reading about. I could pronounce the words, that's all. I didn't get very much arithmetic in my class. We did addition and multiplication but didn't do very much with fractions. Addition and multiplication and division was about the most we did. If a child could count up to one hundred, they will pass a grade.

After supper Grandfather took us up on the hill. Then he talked to us and asked us if we were going to school that next day. We told him no, that the next day was Saturday. Now, the old man was anxious to learn to try to pronounce the English words after we said them. We would teach him, "Today is Friday, tomorrow is Saturday, and then Sunday." He could always say Sunday, but Saturday was very hard for him to say, so he would say *hutudu*. He would hold up his fingers and count, "First school day, second school day, third school day, fourth school day, fifth school day, hutudu, Sunday."

We told him we were not going to school on hutudu. We told him we have to work in the morning; we have to do our chores. Everybody has to do something on hutudu. We would carry wood, haul water, or clean up the grounds. When Saturday morning came around, all the boys were working to do what they could to clean up the school ground and fill up the wood boxes in the employees' houses. After lunch we would be free. Grandfather says we will go up on a hill.

So we went up on the north side of the canyon, but we didn't go very far. We just sat around up there on the rocks, and he was telling us what he knew about Hopi traditions, all about what may come to pass or what already had come to pass. He really wasn't sure what the wonders were, or really didn't know when such things will come around. It might be during his lifetime, his children's lifetimes, or during his grandchildren's lifetimes.

"Now the elders used to tell us that the Bahana will come. He might be a dark bahana. The people will not know or will not recognize who this person might be. He might be white, just like these people that are here now. But the Bahana is supposed to have a great knowledge of wisdom that he was to come and teach the people—the truth. If he should find us all wicked, then he will not hesitate to do away with the wicked, because we are told that we will be branded. This is hard for me to understand. The only thing that I have been going by, now, is what has already come to pass. So it is the desire of all the Hopi people that you, our children, must go to school and learn to speak the white man's language. But it is my doubt, or anybody else's doubt, that if one goes to school he will become as wise as these white people are.

"The people like myself that have heard this story of traditions will watch the children that are now going to school very closely, for we see this school has been started. Men like myself, judges from every village, have been to Fort Defiance and have come face to face with the white man and discussed this matter. We have given our consent that the school will be established here. The white man said that if the school should be established and the children go to school and learn to speak and write the English language, they will become our leaders, that they will be able to compete with the white man. At that time it was decided that every clan among the Hopi people must be represented by a child from his group at the school. You must understand that all the children that are here at school now are not just anybody, but they are representing each clan from all the villages. But I think the time will come that every family's child will be going to school. Right now the agent here is just kind of going easy, but I think that it won't be very long before all the children will be in the school.

"Whatever you do here at school, try to learn all you can, because you have only a limited time. It has been agreed upon that every child must only come four years, but I don't know how long that will stand, because I see that every so many years a new agent comes in, and it seems like each one of them has come with different ideas. When your time is up, you might see you have to go to school some more, which is what I want you to do, because I want you boys to learn something."

After he was telling us this, we saw that it was getting late, that he would like to go home. We didn't know how late it was, so we went down to the school. Grandfather went into the kitchen and asked the cook for lunch that he could take along. The cook gave him a big loaf of bread and a good-sized piece of meat. He put this lunch into a sack and put it around back of his back and started home.

Grandfather would come to see us like that much oftener from then on until cold weather set in. Then it was near Christmas. This was my first Christmas, and I didn't really know what was going to happen. All the rest of the children who had been there seemed very happy because they are expecting some presents, like what they were given the year before.

On Christmas Eve all the kids were yelling and pointing up to the top of the mesa. I ran around to the back of the building and looked up on top of the mesa, and there was Santa Claus. He had a burro saddled up, and he was trying to drive the burro off the sheer bluff. This was one of the Hopi men, because he has seen the Santa Claus played by some white man.

They must have cut up a lot of paper, because he just had bushels of it. He was on the highest point on the mesa. He would take hold of a bunch of paper and just hold it out over the bluff, and when he let it go the papers would be flying everywhere in the sky. Everybody was out, and the children were trying to catch these flying papers as they came near to the ground.

This burro he had was a pinto burro. After he had thrown down all his papers, he couldn't make the burro come down, so he took the saddle off and wrapped it up in a blanket and threw it down. So then he tried to get off the bluff, but he had to walk around back and forth, and somebody had to go up and lead him to the trail. He was sort of clowning up all this, because he knew the trail. He came down and had just pockets and pockets all over filled with candy. This was my first candy. He was masked with a regular Santa Claus mask. He had the regular suit on. That was the first Santa Claus I ever did see.

All this time nobody knows that they were putting up a Christmas tree and hanging the presents over in the schoolhouse. The schoolhouse was just one building, sort of like a chapel. Anyway, Santa Claus was just giving away one stick of candy to each child, because there isn't enough to go around. There were about a hundred children at that time.

Everybody was excited that evening. About eight o'clock they get all the children lined up, and we marched up to the schoolhouse. When we got in, there was a big Christmas tree. Everybody was seated. We sang some songs. I wish I could have remembered one of the songs, but it was one of those old-fashioned Christmas hymns. After a few songs were sung, some children had Christmas pieces. I didn't know those children had been practicing on pieces all that time to have a little entertainment.

After the Hopi children got through, then Santa Claus came in. Every child was given everything alike so that no names were on the packages. The same way with the girls. Old Santa didn't have to look for any names but just passed them out.

Just as soon as we receive our presents we would open them up to see what the Santa Claus had given us. There was marbles and gloves and handkerchiefs and candy and scarfs and pocketknives and both kinds of Jew's harps for the boys.

The girls got dolls, aprons, capes, handkerchiefs, and I don't know what else. After all the presents were given out, we went back to the dormitories, and everybody was afraid somebody might steal their presents, so some of us took our presents to bed.

The next day was Christmas Day, and everybody was out playing marbles. Before noontime many of them didn't have any marbles. They didn't have anything left, because they just gambled with the marbles. Then if they lose all their marbles, they trade what they have to get the marbles back. I know I did that, but the knife I never would give away. That is one thing I kept.

I thought I was going to keep that knife all the time, but someone went through my bed one night and stole the knife. I had kind of an idea who it was, but I didn't say anything about it. About a week after that, I started crawling around myself at night. When I reached into the pants pockets, I found about at least eight knives in one pocket, so I took the whole bunch of them and went back to bed.

The next morning I was up good and early and was already dressed when the door was opened up to let us out. Just as soon as I got out through the door I went straight for the wash. I got into the river and took the knives out of my pocket and looked at them. Sure enough, one of them was mine. So I put my knife in my pocket and buried the rest of them.

During that day and afternoon while the school was in session, I knew the boy that had taken the knives was in school, so I went back and took the knives out of the ground and took them to the disciplinarian. I handed the knives to him. He asked me where I got them, and I told him I found them. He told me that I couldn't find seven knives all at one time, and then of course I felt kind of guilty. I went around and found one of the older boys that can speak English. By that time he knew the truth, and I took him around to this man, so he explained to him how I got these knives and how I had found my own knife with the bunch.

That evening when the boys lined up to go to supper, the disciplinarian held out the knives in front of them and told the boys that whoever has missed his knife sometime ago may come and see if they can recognize the knives as theirs. The boys went up one by one. It was surprising how many boys had missed their knives. There wasn't enough for them to go around. He then asked the boys to take everything out of their pockets so he could come along and see. When the boys took their things out of their pockets, they laid them down on the ground, and the disciplinarian went through the boys' pockets anyway. He found two or three knives on certain ones, so some of those boys had been crawling nights. I don't know just how the guilty ones felt about it, but the disciplinarian never would tell the boys where he got the first bunch of knives.

After that time I went back to school every year, after having my vacation at home. What vacation I had would be spent herding sheep or watching the fields. Every time when the school is closed, the people or men will go or come in to the school to get their children, and there would be the great excitement of coming home. Any boy that had a well-to-do father would always have a horse to ride home. After starting out, the boys would come together and would either run races or hunt rabbits, chasing after jackrabbits. I was old enough then that I could ride pretty good.

During one of these summers we were taking care of the horses, I and Kachina. We were supposed to be taking turns, but when we got down to the field we would both go after the horses. My father had a good bunch of horses. He had them running in with another man's bunch. We used to get them corralled up and would then get a horse each and get down into the bottom of the wash and race the horses. We don't want anybody to see us, so we got down to the bottom of the wash.

One day we drove the horses up to the lake, where there was water in a natural tank. The weather had been good, and it had rained that summer, and the lake was full, and we drove our horses up there. We were always riding the best runners. We got up there and looked across and saw that an old coyote was getting a drink. We knew the other horses would go home by themselves, so we stopped and watched the coyote.

It would stop for a while and then go back again for another drink. We thought he was getting good and full. After he had enough water, he started off, and off we went after this old coyote. The coyote was so full of water he wasn't going very fast. We caught up with him in a short while. We were on horseback and almost on top of him, so we thought we would get off the horses and catch him ourselves.

So we jumped off and started after him on foot. He left us behind. So we went back and got on the horses and chased after him again. We drove the horses after that old coyote until it was completely played out. We killed it and went back to the water.

We killed him by beating him up with our sticks. We always had carried sticks for weapons. That was, we carried those sticks, two or three of them, right in the front. There will be a string of cloth or band doubled because it will hold the sticks, and it would cross in front where we kept them. We carried them for weapons. They were greasewood sticks, about one-half or one inch around. We also carried them when we were walking, and we also had our bows and arrows. If you are carrying a bow and arrows, there will be only two or three, because if you have a bunch in your hand, you will drop them. We would throw at the rabbits from horseback and would try to hit them any way we can. With practice, a man would get expert at hitting rabbits on the run with a stick and also with an arrow.

When we get back to the water, we get off the horses, and they were sweating badly. We didn't know what to do, because when my dad sees the horses sweating he would sure know they had been running someplace. So we rode them into the water and got off and washed them off. Then we took them out, and the horses rolled over in the sand to dry off. We were riding bareback. We always rode bareback. It is best that way, because if the horse fell—getting his foot into a prairie dog hole—there is no danger that you will stay in the saddle. You just fly off about ten feet from the horse as he rolls over in the sand. Anyway, the horse could dry with the sand, so we rubbed them off with our hands, and they were just as clean as they were before. Ever since then, taking the horses to water, we would always stop to see if there was another coyote there, but that was the only one that we ever caught.

That fall we went back to school again, and that year was Kachina's last year. That was his fourth year, and it was my third year. After we went back to school, everything went as usual. We were getting used to this schooling, and there didn't seem anything very exciting, the same old thing over again. Like Christmas, just always one more exciting event that will happen. I don't remember if there was any New Year's or Thanksgiving. Christmas was the only thing that every child looked for, and also, of course, when it comes time to come home for vacation.

When that year of school was out, I came home again on our vacation. I was old enough then that I could take care of my own horses or my father's horses, so during that summer I didn't spend much time with my uncle. But along in the summer I missed him. My grandfather had sent him down to Phoenix with the rest of the boys. It happened that somebody came up from Phoenix, a school employee, at least I think he was sent out to get some pupils from the Hopi country. My grandfather thought it was a good idea and sent his son on down there.

That fall I went back to school by myself. When I was there for a while, a bunch of Walpi men came through and said they were going over to Zuni to see the Shalako Ceremony.[34] After those men went over there, they heard that there was smallpox over there. They must have been there by that time and couldn't do anything about it.

Just about that time my grandfather came to see me. He got there late in the afternoon, driving a burro. Just as soon as I saw him he told me that he was there to take me home.

"Why?"

"I just thought that you might want to come out and visit for a while."

"Why?"

"We heard about the smallpox, and the smallpox is a very bad thing. It will kill a lot of people, so I thought that I would come in and take you out home for a few days. Because if that smallpox ever gets over here in the villages, you won't see some of those people."[35]

Grandfather said he was going up to the superintendent to ask him to let me go home. We had our supper there and left right after supper. We drove the burro ahead of us. I must have walked about three miles and then got on the burro, and my grandfather was coming behind, driving it. We were coming by way of Polacca. We came by the Walpi point, and he drove the burro back up into the hills among those rocks, and then he said that we were going just there, that was as far as we are going to go. We are going to rest there until the next morning.

There was a house there. When we got there, I got off the burro

---

34. This Zuni event is similar to some Hopi Kachina ceremonies.

35. Apparently the smallpox scare made it easier for the grandfather to remove Edmund from school for the special baptism he had arranged for him.

and my grandfather opened the door. I saw that there was quite a number of people in there. They welcomed us like they were expecting us. I don't know just what time of the night it was, but it was kind of late. They gave us mutton stew to eat, which they had prepared for that occasion. I don't know what there was there, but there were quite a few men there and only one woman.

Just as soon as we ate, the woman cleared away the food, and it being a Hopi custom, they all started to smoke their pipes. I was tired and sleepy, but my grandfather asked me not to sleep. They wanted me to stay up. Afterwhile they used up all the tobacco in their pipes—native tobacco. After a while one old man asked the woman to get the bowl ready and make some soapsuds or lather out of the soapweed. She says, "I have already got the soapweed soaking, so it is ready now. The only thing I have to do is stir it up."

"All right, you better get busy because it is late, and the boy is sleepy. Just as soon as we get through, we're all going to bed."

The woman got the bowl out, and I saw that the soapweed was in the water. She went to work and got the soapweed out and cut them up or tore them up in strips. She started stirring with her hands, and soon the suds started coming up and filled the bowl. She worked and worked until she got it fine and soft and then took it all out. Then the old man says to another man, "All right, it is your turn to attend to the boy."

He stepped forward and said, "All right, young man, step forward. Don't be scared, this isn't anything. We are not going to hurt you. We will wash your head first, and then we will afterwards tell you what this is all about."

Grandfather said, "Don't be scared now, Son. Nobody will hurt you."

I got up and took my coat off. It was canvaslike clothing that the government used to order. This man took me by the hand and led me up to the bowl and asked me to stoop over. I was told not to be scared, but I was shivering. The man had an ear of white corn and used that on my head, dipping it in the suds and using it on my head four times and then laid it aside and used his hands. After he got through, he asked the rest to come and do the same. They all had their hands on my head, but the first one was the only one that used the white ear of corn.

After everybody was through, this man stepped forward again and took a handful of fine cornmeal and rubbed it on my face. He took hold of this ear of corn, and with that he went up and down on my breast. At last he said, "From now on your name is such and such," and he explained what the name meant. Each one said that we shall remember and will always call him by that name.

This time the man that washed my head wrapped me up in a blanket and set me by the fireplace. I was not cold, but I was scared and was shivering from being scared. Then all the men filled up their pipes again and started smoking again. After they had used up all their tobacco in their pipes, they all turned around to where I was and asked my grandfather to tell me what this was all about.

My grandfather said, "Now, Son, as I have already told you, this is as far as we are going. The reason that I went in to the school to get you is to bring you here so these people here will do what they have done. Now we had been wondering for a long time who to select for our purpose. That is, that we would like to have someone that we can really depend on to learn this bahana language, because the knowledge that has been handed down to us from our elders, from our ancestors from one generation to the other by way of mouth, has told us that the Hopi and the bahana are not friends. They are not friends, by all means, but they are brothers and are supposed to be on an equal basis in life. We have been wishing, all of us, and hoping all this time, in fact in a good part of our lives, that we could see the true Bahana come, as it is our belief that whenever he comes, he will teach us his knowledge. He will know us all by heart, and the wicked ones he will execute by beheading them. After doing away with all the wicked, he will beautify our land and make it new. From then on the righteous people will live forever. Those are our wishes. We have been wondering about this for a long time. It is for this reason that you are being baptized here this night. From now on, if you will really understand what we are selecting you for, you must never be afraid of anything.

"I have told you before that there are no such things as two-spirited people. Such people are said to be witches who can transform themselves into different animals or birds. You cannot be expected to understand everything tonight, but later on as you see things happen you will know why we wanted you to go and learn all you can about the truth. It has been told to us that when this Bahana comes to us, there will be no more sickness. If there is, his touching hand will be healing. When he comes, there will be no more medicine men among the Hopi because the medicine men cannot compete with the true Bahana. That is all I will tell you tonight, but as the days go by I will tell you a few things whenever I have a chance, because there is a great deal to be learned. You must learn both sides, otherwise you will never find out who is right and what the truth is in this world."

The other men answered him, "Yes, that is how it shall be and will be."

While Grandfather was telling me this, I was pretty sleepy. When he got through talking to me, we went to bed. The next morning this man that had given me the baptizing took me out toward the rising sun and told the sun the name he had given me, which is the Hopi custom. They will always tell the sun the name that they have given to people when they are babies or when they are grown. This sort of an affair is natural, having babies to be named and then taking them out before the rising sun and telling the names to the sun. But with the older people, when they are initiated into the ceremony, the new person getting into the ceremony must choose their godfather. Then when they are baptized they will always go out in the morning and tell their new name to the sun. Whenever this sort of thing is done to the person, they tell his new name to the sun and are supposed to forget his old name. When those that know your new name call you by that name after that, that is how everybody will learn and find out that you have a new name. I never was called by this new name because I went back to school and didn't stay around with these friends of my grandfather.

After having breakfast that morning, instead of taking the home way, Grandfather took me right back to school. Anyway, these people had given me some piki and parched corn to take back with me. On our way back to school I asked my grandfather who the men were. He said that the old man who lives there is his friend and also told me the name of the man that baptized me.

After that time my grandfather would be coming into Keams Canyon about twice a month. He would be telling me about the Hopi traditions, all the theories about what is going to come to pass.

During that year, these men that had gone to Zuni returned, and not long after their coming back the smallpox broke out. The first victim was a man by the name of Tufci. It soon spread all over the Walpi village and then over to Second Mesa. By this time the whole reservation was condemned. They had to draw the line between the school and the Hopi village. There were guards going back and forth day and night. No one could come in to the school from the Hopi villages.

I could not see my grandfather during the months of December, January, February, and March, not until about the last of April. By that time the Hopi towns were all fumigated, and the people that had the disease and still survived were bathed in chemicaled water, and all the clothing and everything they had was burned. This was done by the Agency.

I was surprised to see my grandfather coming in to the school with good, decent clothes, because the old man was always saving, and he usually had many patches on his clothes, especially on his pants. There would be more patches on his knees. He never realized how heavy this made his pants because he was used to it.

He was also wearing shoes, where he usually wore moccasins. The Hopi started wearing moccasins when they learned to tan hides, after the Spaniards had introduced cattle into this country. Before that time they always wore sandals. I knew where there were some sandals in a cave. I have seen them many times. But at that time I didn't have any interest in collecting relics. They were old Hopi sandals made out of yucca. What they did on the bottom was put pine gum and then walk on the sand. There were three pairs in the cave.

Later in the day there were more people coming in. I didn't know, but they had been invited by the Agency to come in to the school for a feast. We didn't notice, but something like three heads of beef were killed. I knew quite a number of girls and boys were busy making bread. There was quite a bunch of people came in that afternoon.

It was rather a sad night, because when these people came in they had told us the news about the people who have passed away with smallpox. I was lucky that my parents had only a light touch of smallpox. My mother had only one spot on her breast, and my father had a spot in the palm of each of his hands. Two of my aunts died with smallpox: Vivian's mother and my father's sister.

My grandfather told me all the news regarding his family and my family. He also told me that my father and mother were again driven out of the clan house and that they are not living there anymore, which was a good thing, my grandfather said.

The next day the Hopi had the feast at the Agency. Some of us children were given permission to go home and visit around. I wanted to see my family and find out where they were living. Some of these people that had smallpox were very hard to recognize. Their faces were all speckled and they looked awful.

When I got home, I found my parents still in Shipaulovi, living in the neighbors' house next door, on the right side of the clan house. I stayed three days and went back to school again. That was the last I saw of my parents for a long time.

9

School in Phoenix

Shortly after I went back to school at Keams Canyon, there was a lady came up from the boarding school at Phoenix after some more children. Must be about sixteen of the children thought they would like to go down to Phoenix. So they were sent home to see their parents, to see if they might get their consent to go away to school.

This was my last year in school, the fourth year, and I didn't have any thought of going away to school. But when these children got home, my grandfather heard about it, so he followed these children back into the canyon, and Vivian was one of them. This was about the twenty-ninth of April, 1899. Just as soon as he got there to the school, he got hold of me and took me by the hand straight up to the agent. When he got into the office, he told the agent that I was going away with the rest of the children, down to Phoenix.

The agent looked at me and says, "Do you want to go to school at Phoenix?"

"I don't know."

"Well, your grandfather says you are going."

"He said I am going, and if he says so, I'll go."

We had everything settled, and my grandfather took me up on the hill. I was expecting to have him tell me some more of what he would like to have me do. We sat down on a rock.

"Son, I think it is a good time and chance for you to go away to school. This is your last year here, and I am giving you four years more to go to school somewhere else. Whatever you do when you get down there, do the best you can. See what you can learn, but first of all my advice is to choose that book of knowledge which holds the truth of what I have been telling. The book that holds the truth is a black book, and it is about that thick. The white people keep it at the bottom of the pile, where Hopis cannot see it. If we ever learn the truth of this book, then we can compete with the white man. This is why he is afraid to teach us right now. This is the truth that I want to know.

"You know that on the east of Mishongnovi there is a mission. I am the man that had given my consent to the white man to build a house there. When they came to me, they told me that when they built that house they will take care of the old people and poor people, and make them clothes and give them baths once in a while and feed them. That is all that I was told.

"I am getting old and can't go much farther. I thought I might have a chance to live there, but I went to that place the other day and there were people talking every day, telling something that I didn't understand. They told me that it was the true knowledge that they had brought to us. They said that when you are baptized into this religion you are not going to hell. They said that you are going to heaven, but I doubt it. They said that hell is a firepit where the bad people will be thrown in.

"Hearing all this, I wanted to go further into it, that I might understand and find out the truth. But how will I ever do it? You have to go, and be sure to choose this book and find out all you can about the truth. But one thing that you must never do: don't ever get baptized into this thing until you bring me back the truth. Because I see now that whoever talks or teaches this, as they are doing over here, there is a lot of bait thrown out, I find. A lot of sweet talk. Don't ever believe it! If this is the truth here that they have been talking to me about, and if this same thing is in this book that I have spoken of, I want to know first, and I will not be forced into it. When I am convinced that this is the truth, then it will be my consent, and you and I will then be baptized. Don't ever let anyone lead you into this thing to be baptized without my consent. I am your father and you have to listen to me.

"Our ancestors say the Hopi is looking for this Bahana who never was baptized after his death. Now in this religion these people would only sprinkle you with holy water, like people charming themselves against death. Every Hopi is being baptized, but we are only baptized to try to do right. But who has followed what they had pledged to do at the time they are baptized? I know that I am a sinner. Every soul in this world is a sinner. That is the reason we are looking for the truth. We are all blamed with a sin. We are told that when this Bahana comes, he may come with a mirror. He will take a person and turn a mirror on them, and if you are a witch and look into that mirror you will see whatever animal or insect you have turned yourself into. There will be no trouble for this Bahana to pick out his enemy or the wicked people. He will know us all.

"Don't forget what I am sending you down there for. And if that book really contains the truth, you will surely learn something. And when you do, come back someday and study the people here. Study the Hopi and get into all the ceremonies. Don't be afraid to initiate into them. Find out all you can and listen to everything that is being done or said in any ceremony. Now, you have already been initiated into my Kachina ceremony, and you have seen what we did. What we have done, we told our novices—you were one of them—that what you had seen there, we told you that was the truth. We told you that the Kachina are supernatural beings, but they're not, and all the ceremonies are like that. In a way, every ceremony is devious.

"The different clans who have taken up these ceremonies have passed away, one after another. The day will come when all my relatives will vanish. When that day comes, no matter where you go—to Walpi, Second Mesa, Third Mesa—you will find that clans that support different ceremonies will be vanishing. If this was the true way, the clans that have carried these ceremonies should be the only ones to prosper, and the poor people who never had any ceremonies would have vanished long ago because they would have had no god. But this is not the way it is. All these traditions have been handed down during many, many years from one generation to the other, and up to this day all these things are all vague in our minds."

After telling me all this, he got right up. "Son, I will have to go. I would hate to see you get in the wagon and start off. I may not be brave enough at the last minute to see you go away. I don't want to shed my tears. I hate to see you go. I don't like to see you go, but for the benefit of the people, you must go. Always remember what I have taught you. Before you ever touch any food, before you taste any food, always remember what to say. It is the only thing that I was taught when I was young, and here I am. There must be something to it, because now I am getting old. Make up your mind to be happy to go, and I will feel the same."

When he said this, we both got up and started down the hill. After we got down to the school it was getting late, but anyways, he said that he had to go. So we went into the kitchen and they packed him some lunch and he started out. The last thing he did before he left, he hugged me and shook hands with me, and started down the road.

The next day was the day that we were going away. We made ready, and the man that was going to take us to the railroad got into Keams Canyon that evening. The next day was the first of May, 1899. We were loaded on a covered wagon and started out of the canyon. As we went over the hill, I looked back at what I thought would be my last look upon the Keams Canyon School. The old cottonwood trees were just about starting to leaf, and they looked yellowish green.

I was the only boy with the six girls going down to the railroad at Holbrook. We were two days on the road to Holbrook. We made camp at the trading post site at the foot of the mountain east of the Indian Wells trading post. I was curious all this time because I never was that far away from home. Before supper was ready, I started climbing up the mountain, and I went to the top. I didn't care for supper; I was exploring the country. Just before sundown I started down. The girls thought I had run away. They were looking around the place at the bottom of the mountain when I got to them. Vivian was about to cry. She was carrying my lunch. She had come out looking for me with my lunch.

The next day we went on to Holbrook. We got there quite late. There was only the station and trading post and one store. That was the whole town. That evening the train came by. That was the first train and locomotive that I ever did see in my life.

That night at Holbrook we were told that we were to be up early because the train was due just at that time. I really didn't know what time it was, but anyway I was told to be up pretty close to sunrise. Of course, there was not much of any accommodations there. The girls that were with me, the lodging that they had was in an old shack, and I was in an old Navajo hogan.[36] Early the next morning we were waking up, and as I have said before, there are no accommodations and none of us had even washed our faces. The lady that was taking us only had brought us some crackers and a can of sardines for each of us, and some water. That was our breakfast.

Soon the train had come. We walked up to the train. I was rather a little scared of getting on the train. The coaches at that time had an open space between connections, and in trying to go in from one

36. A hogan is a traditional Navajo dwelling still in use in many areas of the Navajo reservation. Typically it is octagon-shaped and made of rough timbers and branches, and covered with earth.

coach to the other, you have to hold on to your hat for fear that the wind will blow it off. After we were all seated and the train started to pull out, I was looking out through the window, and it wasn't sunlight yet. I just kept looking out of the window to see all I can.

Soon we were coming in to another town, and at this time the sun was just coming over the horizon. The train stopped. I looked out, and we all looked out, and we saw a sign that says Winslow. Then we started on again. From there on we could see the mountains which I was used to seeing from the Hopi villages, especially the San Francisco Peaks. We were coming nearer to the peaks all the time. There must have been a lot of curves on this railroad all the time. Where I was sitting I would see the mountains from my side of the train. Then once in a while I would be seeing the mountains from the other side. Every once in a while the engine would blow a whistle. Now, getting around the San Francisco Peaks, we stopped again. We all looked out and saw the sign that says Flagstaff.

Then we went on through the tall pine trees. On account of the trees I could not see much of the country. Every once in a while I would be looking back to see if I could still see the San Francisco Peaks. Then we stopped again and saw a sign that says Williams. All this time I was counting the stops. Then we went again and made another stop. This one was Ash Fork. There we had our dinner, which was much better eats than we had in the morning. Then we were told that we have to wait two hours for another train, and I thought it would be a good chance to climb around the rocks. I went around to try and find the highest point around there to see if I could see the San Francisco Peaks, but I saw that we had gone too far and were too low.

Finally the train came. We got on board again and went on. Sometime in the afternoon we made another stop, and this was at Prescott. By this time I was very much uneasy, because I wanted to take a rest and didn't know where to go. I thought I would now have a chance. Just as soon as the train stopped, I jumped off and ran to the bushes. I was hardly getting up when the bell started to ring on the locomotive. I had to run to catch the train. Just before I got there the train started to move, and the porter saw me coming and ran toward me and got ahold of me and swung me on to the steps and pushed me on. When I got in the coach, the girls asked me where I had been, and I told them that I had to get off. They understood why I had to get off. No one had told me that there was a washroom on the train. Only the girls had been told.

From then on I forgot all about the stops, and I was very interested in seeing the country. I noticed that we were going down lower and lower all the time. Just about sundown we stopped again, and we were told that we were going to have supper there. This place was Wickenburg. After supper we got on the train again. The trains must have been going pretty slow in those days, because here it was the fourth or fifth of May, and getting on the train at sundown we were told that we were due in Phoenix at nine o'clock. Well, it got dark, and then I had to close my window, and wondered in what sort of place I will wake up in the morning.

At last the porter came in and yelled "Phoenix!" and the train came to a stop. We got off the train and there was somebody to meet us. He took us around to a big wagon or hayrack, and we all climbed up on the wagon and started out. It seemed like we had a long ride. I will never forget how the hayrack rattled and how the horses would trot. I had only seen a little bit of a town, and after we passed the lights it was all dark. All this time I had in mind that we were going to a place where there might be big houses several stories high, but when we got there we stopped in front of tents. I got off the wagon and was taken to one of the tents and was told that I would sleep there.

It was so hot that I couldn't go to sleep. Not only that, there was a lot of mosquitoes, and I don't believe that I had much to eat that night. Early in the morning I heard the sound of the bugle, which I will never forget. Never saw so many boys and girls! They were all lined up to go to breakfast. Being a newcomer, I didn't get in line but was looking on. That was the first time I heard the band play *The Star Spangled Banner*.

Then we marched up to the dining room and I was placed at a table, but every once in a while I seemed to be just swinging back and forth. I wanted to sit down, but they have to go through a ceremony of saying grace before eating or sitting down. Finally we sat down. I was kind of thirsty, so the first thing I went for was water. I only had a taste of it, and I couldn't drink it because it was so salty. Then I thought that I might drink some coffee, but that was still worse. I was with my uncle then—Edwin. He was sitting beside me, and I asked him if somebody might have poured salt into the coffee by mistake.

"No, the water is salty."

Well, I didn't eat very much that morning.

After we got out, my uncle was given permission to take me around and entertain me that day. I was still thirsty and I wanted a drink, so he told me that there was a river, by which he meant a canal. This was only half a mile away, so we went down to this canal and I had my drink there, which tasted much better. Every time when I got thirsty I would run for the canal. Soon I got tired of running to the canal, so I got me an old lard can and used to go down there and carry water and keep it in my tent. But you can't keep no water there because it gets so hot. It is like drinking hot water. I couldn't eat anything. Just at that time the apricots were ripe, and we used to go out to the nearby orchard and get some apricots.

Of course, what money I had I tried to make it last as long as I could. The money that my grandfather had given me was a dollar, and at the Agency they gave me another dollar. The first two dollars that I ever had in my pocket—silver dollars.

For the first few days I was homesick. My uncle would take me around places close to school. I knew I had to be like the rest of the boys. I was then acquainted with several of them. I had a great desire to be a man and not be homesick all the time. The first two Sundays while we were at the canal swimming, they offered me some tobacco, but I didn't want to take a bite. One day my uncle said, "Ed, if you are ever going to be a man and do away with your homesickness, learn to smoke and chew tobacco."

I asked him if the smoking or chewing will make me sick.

"No. It is the only way you can become a man."

So, on the third Sunday, Edwin took his gang down to the canal. I noticed that the boys were kind of organized in different gangs. They say that I never can be a man unless I chew and smoke tobacco like they do. Finally I decided I would chew tobacco.

They had a brand of chewing tobacco that was called the Golden Rope. I took a bite of it, and I didn't have it in my mouth very long before the saliva came out from all sides of my mouth. It got so full I could hardly spit it out, so I just poured it out. I felt all right. They didn't know that I had got rid of the tobacco. Then they found out that I wasn't chewing it, so they gave me another bite. This time they were watching me very closely. I wasn't chewing on it; I was just holding it in my mouth. At first the tobacco was just burning hot in my mouth. I couldn't help but swallow some of it, and in no time I was sick. I had gotten sick because of the tobacco and also from the heat. It was so hot!

It was time for us to go back, but I was so sick I couldn't get up and couldn't walk. I was drunk from tobacco more than I was sick. My uncle carried me up to the school and put me to bed. The next morning I was all right. But still my head was swimming. I didn't want to have any more tobacco, but Edwin insisted that I would soon get used to it. Of course, I wanted to be a man like they were, so I went on until I got used to it. I guess that was the first "good" habit I formed with the boys.

I really had a hard time getting interested in girls. When I arrived in Phoenix, the first thing I knew was that some girl wanted to talk to me. I was shy, so the first morning when we went to school I went to the second grade classroom and was given a desk to sit at. Right across the aisle from me was a girl. She kept looking at me, and every once in a while she would wink her eye. I just pretended that I did not see her. She was a Pima. This morning she had been doing that, but I was so shy I did not want the teacher to notice me. The teacher just kept looking at the girl but did not say anything to her that morning.

The next morning we went to school again. When we got inside, I sat down. She slipped a note right on top of my desk, and I just stared at it. I noticed the teacher had seen what she was doing. She called to her and said, "Amy, please don't bother the boy. He is new, and he does not know you, and he probably does not like to be bothered. If you think that you want to make love to him, just wait a while until he gets really acquainted."

Everybody turned around and was looking at us. I had my eyes on the note, but I did not want to pick it up. So the teacher walked over to me and said, "Ed, just pick the note up and put it in your pocket and read it after you get out."

I did not want to pick the note up, so I just pushed it up to the end of my desk and left it there. But it seemed as though every eye was on me, so then after a while I got up nerve enough to pick it up. After school I went over to the boys' building and read the note. It said, "Ed, would you like to be my friend? I wish you would. Answer my note if you please. Amy S." I did not want to answer the note, and of course I felt that I did not want to be bothered with any girl, so I never did answer the note.

Most every day she would slip a note into my desk. The note would read, "When are you going to make up your mind to be my friend? A. S." One day I picked up the note and added to it another S. I just left it there. And when we were going out after class, someone picked it up and left it on the teacher's desk. The teacher was a young lady, an Oklahoma Indian. She probably read the note.

The next morning we went back to school, and the teacher had put the note into her own desk. When we got in, before we start our work, the teacher called, "Attention, please." Everybody sat up. "Now, what I want to say is that I do not like to have any of you girls send any notes to any of these boys. Here is a note that was written to Ed. Someone picked it up and put it on my desk. I will read it to you. 'Ed, dear. You do not know that I love you, but I really do. Yours as ever, A.S.S.'"

The whole class just laughed. Then the teacher said, "Now, Amy, that is just what you are making yourself into. I don't think that boy came down here to make love to the girls. He came down here to go to school."

That Pima girl, she kept on nevertheless. Nothing would embarrass her. After two years' time I still won't have a thing to do with her. At the end of two years she was my worst enemy.

When school let out for vacation, the local Pimas, Maricopas, and Papago went home. There were only a few of the boys and girls left. What we did, we worked in the morning and then lay around in the afternoon. It was so hot! I wanted to do something, but being a newcomer, they would not let me go anywhere to try to find any work. But just about three weeks before the school began again, my uncle Edwin was working someplace, and one day he told me that the man needed an extra boy. So we went and asked the disciplinarian for permission that I might go out with Edwin. I was granted the permission.

So we would go out early in the morning. We had to walk three miles out into the country. Here we needed to pump the water to irrigate with. We would take turns working on the pump. In those days, fifty cents a day was good pay. At this place we were making twenty-five cents an hour because we had to work the pump so hard, because it was so heavy. Working eight hours a day, we were making two dollars a day.

When school started we didn't have to go anymore. We had a little money saved up. It wasn't given to us, but they put it in the office for safekeeping. In fact, none of the boys were allowed to have too much money to carry around. If you would need a little money, you had to fill out an application blank in order to get any.

Then school started again. That year I was classified, from where I was going to begin. In the Keams Canyon School I was in the third grade, but I started school in Phoenix in the second grade because I couldn't speak English very well. In order to answer anyone in English, I had to line the words out in my mind before I could answer. These children had to talk English among themselves because they were from many different tribes. For example, the boys in Edwin's gang included a Shoshone from Nevada, a Klamath from California, a Hupa from California, and a Walapai.

This gang had a password for chewing tobacco: snipe. When one of us wants to chew tobacco, we would say, "Have to get a snipe." We used to have them hidden away. But smoking got so bad on the school grounds that one day they had all the boys line up, from Company A down to Company D. They found tobacco on almost every one of them. They got some wood and built a fire in front of them, and there was the boys in a line watching it burn up all their tobacco.

All this time, on Sundays, Edwin had been going to a special session of a Bible class. All of a sudden I remember that I was supposed to study that big book that my grandfather had mentioned, so I joined that class. After joining, I used to go to that session every Sunday at two o'clock. At first it was kind of hard for me to understand. In fact, I wasn't speaking English well enough to understand what this was all about. We were doing this for about a year and a half, and then some changes have to be made. That is, the superintendent was transferred. At the same time, the Bible teacher was also transferred. For a while we didn't have any Bible study.

Then we got a new superintendent. The school was bad then, and

I noticed a big difference. The superintendent that we got at this time was very religious and he just put his hands down on everybody, that they all must have Bible study every Sunday afternoon. It used to be that we had Sunday school in the morning, but now every Sunday afternoon we had to go to the schoolrooms, and each teacher had to take up the Bible. This got so it was too monotonous. The young people didn't like it. They used to go off someplace Sunday afternoons to keep away from it.

Another thing was organized; it was this anti-tobacco league. Most of us were forced into it. It was hard, because we all had to sign up for it. In order to smoke or chew, the boys used to go away out to the canal or someplace else. They got so that they would have some cans buried around, containing their tobacco.

It had come around to 1901. There was a man by the name of Dr. Miller who was very much interested in museum business.[37] He had been on the Hopi reservation, and I had met him in Grandfather's field near the only road that used to come from Flagstaff. I had had old school clothes on at the time, so it must have been about 1896. This man was looking for someone to go up with him as an interpreter. He was telling me that he has been on the reservation more than once and that he had met some of the boys. I told him I was one of the boys he had met there in the field when we were looking through those field glasses. Then he recognized me. "Are you Eddie? Well, it would sure be a good thing for you to go back home again and have a nice trip with me."

I was to go up with him that summer. He said that we were going out on a collection trip, to see if we can do some excavating around these old cemeteries. He got permission from the superintendent for me to go. Everything was settled, so we got ready and started up.

37. Dr. Joshua Miller, president of the Arizona Antiquarian Association, died in Flagstaff on July 23, 1901, at the age of fifty-five. A brief obituary note by James Mooney appeared in a 1901 issue of *American Anthropologist* (p. 592).

We had made arrangements with the agent at Keams Canyon to send a team to Holbrook. We asked him not to send anyone until we got to Holbrook and sent him a letter.

We started out on the train, with his wife. Before we started out, he had a little cold. We came up as far as Prescott, and he was getting worse. So we came up here to Flagstaff and he had to stop, and we found out that this cold had developed into pneumonia. They had a place at the Commercial Hotel. He died there within a week, in this hotel. That was in 1901.

That was the summer I started to climb the San Francisco Peaks. I started out with a bicycle that I had rented from a place in Flagstaff and followed this road out. It was more like a trail than a road. At that time there was only one reservoir over here. I went around it, but I couldn't go any further on the bicycle, so I hung it up on a tree and went on. I thought I would climb up and then go back again before breakfast. I don't know how far I went before the trees were so thick I couldn't see anything. I was so hungry and thirsty that I had to turn back. When I came down I couldn't find my bicycle. I forgot where I left it. It wasn't mine and I had to return it. I just kept going. I was hungry.

I got in town late in the afternoon. As I was going along the street I met a man, or somebody spoke to me who had some kind of uniform on. He had one of those old military caps with a straight visor and a round top. He says to me, "Say, young fellow. Where are you from? Aren't you a Hopi boy? I am from Toreva, and I am a teacher out there. My name is Frank Voorhays." He asked me if I knew such and such a man.

"Yes, that is my grandfather."

"Is that really your grandfather?"

"Yes."

"Well, your grandfather has started a trading post there, and I heard him mention you many times. He talks about two boys, Edmund and Edwin, and he says that he started that trading post for you. Oh, he has quite a store. He has been telling me he will make that store for you, and when you come home from school you are to take it on. He has a big idea for you boys.[38] I am going out there just as soon as this man gets here. Who are you with?"

"Dr. Miller. We are going out there to do some collection of some old things. He has started a museum in Phoenix, but he got sick and we have to stay until he gets well."

I had to go back after the bicycle the next morning, and I was lucky enough to find it. It was about due back in this place. It was such a bad mistake that I didn't go out bike riding again that summer.

But in a few days Dr. Miller had died. Mrs. Miller asked me if I wanted to go out to the reservation. I had to think how I was going to get out there and how I was going to get back to school. It would be hard for me to get out and back again to the railroad station. They had promised to pay all my expenses out there and back to school, but now how would I get that much money? I decided to go back with her to Phoenix. It was about three days after Dr. Miller's death that we went back to Phoenix and buried him down there.

When I got back to Phoenix I went out to work again, downtown for some family, because then I wasn't making as much as I was on the trip. Now I was making $1.50 a day with all my expenses. In those days fifty cents or a dollar was worth something. It isn't worth anything now.

That summer I put some more money into my bank account, so when school started again I had something to depend upon. In those days it wasn't anything like now, with picture shows—movies—and all. If there was anything for city entertainment, it might be a lecture or a vaudeville or something like that.

38. In his account here, Edmund makes no other reference to his grandfather's trading post. It is, however, probably one of those briefly mentioned by Charles E. Burton in his report to the commissioner of Indian affairs dated August 7, 1902.

10

The Runaways

When the changes were made at school, then they made everybody go into the Bible class every afternoon. I didn't pay much attention to it. I got so I was caring more about pitching hay or picking melons some- place, because I wanted to raise the price of my train fare like other Hopi boys who wanted to go home for vacation. In those days we all had to pay our own way back if we wanted to go home over vacation. That was what we were working for.

After school started again, I found out that I had been promoted and was in the same class with my uncle.

One day I suddenly got sick right in the school building, and I knew that there wasn't any restrooms for the students. The only one was in the principal's office, but no one else could use it but the employees or the teachers. I was so sick and the rules were so strict, I knew I would have to get outside. I got up from my desk and handed a note to the teacher saying that I was sick. Then I got out in the hall and just ran outside. I had to go clear over to the boys' building. When I got out of there I felt better and walked back over to the classroom. I had hardly sat down when the principal teacher came and stuck her head in the door and said, "Ed, will you come to my office. I would like to see you."

I got right up and walked in there. I hardly went through the door into her office when Bang! went the ruler across my face. It happened that I got the ruler and pulled it out of her hand and broke it on the table.

"How dare you!"

She locked the door and picked up another ruler. Then I picked up a chair. I couldn't get out because the door was locked. I pretended I was going to sling the chair at her head. But as it went back it went through the window and broke it, so I just jumped out that same window.

I walked straight over to the superintendent's office. The principal was on the phone calling the disciplinarian, but I was one step ahead of her. I got to the superintendent, and he said, "Ed, what can I do for you?"

"I don't know if you can do anything for me or not." By this time there were red lines on my face. I said, "Will you look at my face? I got hit across it."

"Got hit? How?"

"Miss Harvey, the principal teacher."[39]

"If she did that she probably had a good reason. What happened? What had you done?"

"I was sick and had to leave the building. I ran through the hall, but of course I did not make any noise or try to disturb anybody. When I came back she called me in her office and hit me with a ruler. I broke it. She locked the door and picked up another one. I picked up a chair. I didn't want to hurt her, but I swung it through a window, and that's how I got out."

"You mean you broke the hole in the window?"

39. Miss Flora E. Harvey was the principal teacher at the Phoenix Indian School during Edmund's attendance there.

"I said I did. I didn't want to get killed in that office. I didn't intend to hurt the teacher. I wanted to get away from her. One hit was enough for me."

"You just sit there."

He called her over there. Finally she came walking in. Then here comes the disciplinarian. He says, "Miss Harvey, you take a seat over here, and Mr. So-and-So, you take a seat over here." Then he says, "Miss Harvey, had this boy made any trouble over at the school?"

"Yes."

"What was the trouble?"

"Well, he left the school without my permission and ran through the hall."

"Now, Miss Harvey, I would do the same thing if I was as sick as he was. You should have asked him the reason, and he could have explained for himself why he had to do that. But you just got all upset and lost your mind. Now, we can't have things going on like this. You would be in more trouble if you had put his eye out. Now, don't ever hit any child in the building anymore. Whipping a child is just using an iron hand. You must realize that there are a lot of other ways that you can punish the pupils if they make a mistake, but not to hit them across their faces with a ruler like that. Now, from now on both of you understand to keep your hands off the pupils. Give them an extra amount of work for punishment."

They didn't have anything to say. They just listen to the superintendent, and then he says, "You can all be dismissed now."

The principal teacher got up and asked me to go back to the school with her, but I said no, that I would rather go to the boys' building and stay over there. I didn't feel well. I didn't go over to the schoolhouse until the next day.

Ever since then I never could make up with the principal teacher, and I was always thinking of how I could get away from that school. After that I paid more attention to geography lessons, because it is the only way that I can find my way out. I put my whole mind on

Arizona, New Mexico, and California, studying rivers and mountains in order to find the road that I am going to use to get away from here. I checked up on the schedule of trains. Just before Christmas, I thought maybe I could draw more money out because it is going to be Christmas. So I put my application in for twenty-five dollars, but they only gave me twenty. They said that was the limit. I wanted to get away, but I didn't attempt to make a start until after New Years'.

It happened that one of the Hopi boys, named Paul, knew that I was going to try to get away, and he said that he wanted to go with me.

"Now, Paul, you stay here, because you are a pretty nice boy. You are only going because I am going."

"Yes, I want to go with you."

"Have you got any money?"

"I had some before Christmas, but I spent it."

"You can't go with me. I am not going to pay for your meals or your way."

Now, one of Paul's relatives, a Hopi by the name of Edwin, was working for a man who lived right across from the school, a Mr. Trackman by name. Paul went over there and borrowed five dollars from Edwin.

"All right, you will have to stop where your five dollars ends. Now, what I am doing is I am planning to get away from this place. I am not going to be caught. Nobody will catch me, I have got everything figured out. If you are going to stick to me, all right. If not, you better stay here."

"I am going to stick with you."

"Just as soon as it gets dark tonight, we are going. We will go down to the store and buy some lunch and a canteen and fill it up with water. You have to carry your own canteen. I'll carry mine."

We went down and we each got a loaf of bread and some graham crackers and a few cans of sardines. We got a canteen and filled it up with water. We went out south to the main entrance. Just as soon as we got opposite the schoolhouse, we turned in toward the schoolhouse and went from place to place in these conduits, and finally got way back underneath the schoolhouse. We were going to stay right there underneath the school building. It was nice and warm in there because of the steam pipes going back and forth. And earlier I had dragged some gunnysacks in and had a nice bed there already. We slept there, and it was dark as pitch. There was only a ventilator hole or two.

The next morning we didn't have to get up. We didn't have to go to roll call. We had our lunches. We got up about eight o'clock and had our breakfast. When nine o'clock came, we were looking out through that ventilator hole at the children coming to school.

We stayed under that schoolhouse for one week. Once we ran out of food, so we got out and went to this fellow Edwin, and I gave him some money to go down to the store to get us some supplies. They were looking for us all over the country but couldn't find us. We got our supplies and went back under the school.

It happened, though, that Mr. Trackman was the justice of the peace at that time, and he heard that two boys had run off from the school. He asked this fellow Edwin, he says, "Where do you suppose your brother has gone? Wasn't that your brother that came one time? Anyway, I saw you both together."

"Yes."

"Where do you suppose they have gone to now? They have been looking for them all over the country. There was no trace of them."

This fellow Edwin says, "I don't know where he went to. He didn't ever tell me that he was going to run away."

"Now, Edwin, being a brother of yours, don't you think he would write to you from someplace, from where he is? If you do hear where he is, let me know, because I have already heard a good deal about this school and how they have been treating those pupils over there."

The next night Edwin, who knew where we were, came around to the ventilator hole.

"Paul?"

"What do you want?"

"Do you mind if I tell Mr. Trackman where you are? I think he could do something for you."

"Do you think he can? He is the justice of the peace."

"Well, I don't know."

"Maybe you better not tell on us yet." So he went back home.

The next night we came out again and went over to the Trackman place. As we were going through his gate he came driving up in his buggy. He stopped and got off the buggy and came over to us.

"Say, are you the two boys I am looking for?"

I says, "Yes."

"Now you boys come on in the house."

We walked into the house, and he said, "Now there is my horse and buggy outside. I just brought you boys in. I found you way up in the mountains near the mines. Are you boys going to stick to my word?"

"All right."

"I am going over to Mr. Goodman, the superintendent, and I am going to tell him that I brought you boys in tonight.[40] And I am going to fix it so that nobody will ever say anything to you boys, and you will not be punished for it. It is about time that the school employees should wake up and treat you people better than they have been doing."

"All right."

He went on over to see the superintendent. He stayed there about an hour. Then he came back and said, "Now, boys, everything is all right. So if they ever ask any questions, tell them that I brought you

40. Charles E. Goodman became superintendent of the Phoenix Indian School on January 8, 1902.

boys in and that I found you on the Black Canyon road. I told the superintendent that it is pretty cold up there and that you might freeze. I told him that I had talked to you boys and didn't have much trouble persuading you to come back. You boys go on over and report to the superintendent. The disciplinarian will be there, because he called him before I left."

We went on over and knocked on the office door and called his name. As we walked in there, Goodman looked at us and said, "Did you boys have a nice vacation?"

"We went away up near the mountains by the copper mines. It was pretty cold up there."

"Don't you think it's pretty nice to be back down here where it's warm?"

We were sure laughing behind our ears. He said to the disciplinarian, "Now, you take these boys back to their rooms. You know what has happened, and I don't think these boys need to be punished. Let them be with the rest of the boys just like nothing has happened."

They took us back, and the next morning we had to get up early, 5:30 again. From there on we were going to school again, but I never could get over thinking of getting away from that place. I just hated to be down there.

The summer came around. After school was out, I went downtown and worked there for a month. The people happened to be moving away, so I went looking for another job. I found a job in town at a restaurant. It was a dishwashing job. Just so I am not back at the school! I didn't go back to the school nights. The disciplinarian heard about it, that these other people have moved away, and he didn't like my not telling him about it. This was not the same disciplinarian. This was the assistant, and he was a Sioux Indian. He called me up from the school and told me he had got a job out there for me, right across from the school. I went out and asked him where the place was, and he said, "Just across the road."

I went up there. When I got there I saw the lady and asked her if she still wanted to have a boy. She said. "Yes, but you have to eat over at the school and come up here at eight o'clock and work until eleven o'clock, for six dollars a month."

Nothing doing! I was not going to work there. I went back to the school and went to the disciplinarian's office.

"I am not going to work at that place up there."

"Why?"

"I want to work at a place where I can make more. I don't want to work for six dollars a month. What's six dollars a month? Did you ever work for six dollars a month?"

"It was the orders here that you are going to work there. If you are not going to work there, you are not going to work anyplace. You are just going to stay here."

"All right. I am not going to work here at the school, either. I will just lay around."

This was about 10:30. I happened to see Paul, who was an office boy at that time.

"Paul?"

"What do you want?"

"Never mind what I want. I am just going to ask you something. You being an office boy, where do they keep the bank books?"

"Just in there, in one of those drawers."

"Is that drawer ever locked?"

"No, it is open all the time."

"All right, Paul. At noontime I am not going to lunch."

"What are you going to do?"

"I am going to the office and get my bank book."

"All right."

When noon came I didn't go to lunch, and just as soon as everybody had gone in to eat, I went over to the office. I finally found the right drawer. I went over the books and found my book.

Just as soon as I got my book out, it was about ten minutes after twelve noon. The streetcar pulled up and I went straight over there and went to the Home Savings Bank and gave my book to the teller. He looked at me and said, "You want some money?"

"I want my money."

"Okay." He looked the account over and says, "Well, your savings here are $110, and your spending money is only $7.50. I have strict orders, and I can't let you have this savings money, but I can let you have the spending money, just not the savings."

"All right. Just give me my spending money if that's all that I can draw. I would like to have the other, but if you can't do it, there isn't anything I can do about it."

"I just can't do it. If I let you have it, I lose my job here."

With the $7.50, then, I went back and got to the school about 1:15 P.M. As I came in, Paul came arunning and said, "Did you get your money?"

"I sure did."

"I think I'll go with you again this time."

"Are you brave enough to go with me? There is going to be trouble this time. This is not going to be under the schoolhouse this time. Do you think you can make it?"

"Sure."

"All right."

"Tomorrow I'll stay out of lunch and I will get my money."

"All right."

The next day he didn't go to lunch and got his book out from the office and went to town. He only got the same amount as I did. It was funny, but *his* spending money was $7.50 too. His savings were only somewhere around $57. He got his money and came back, and I told him I had been looking the country over.

"Where you been?"

"I have been away on top of the tank up there." They had a high tank for the school water supply, and it was over a hundred feet high. I had been looking the country over from there. I asked Paul if he was working this afternoon.

"No."

"All right, we'll go right now."

I wrote a note to my uncle Kachina and stuck it in his trunk, telling him I was leaving my trunk and the rest of my belongings. I had a 22-caliber rifle, and I was leaving that too. We walked off the school ground, and just as soon as we got out we went west. We went about a half mile to the next road and then south. We went about another mile and then east across Central Avenue, where we could have gone to town. Then we went until we came to the Cave Creek road. We went clear down to the Maricopa depot. We asked them when the train is leaving and found out that it had already gone. They told us that the freight train was pulling out pretty soon. We asked him if we could ride the caboose.

"I don't know. You can ride on top."

"We might just as well ride on top." Before the train started we climbed up on top of the freight car and laid down. It started out at four o'clock sharp from the Maricopa depot. We rode the freight train as far as Tempe. When it stopped there, we got off, because anyway we were far enough away. From there we walked on to Mesa City, about six miles. We got there about ten o'clock. We didn't want to be seen anywhere. We went outside of the town and slept on the river bank.

The next morning we went back into town. The school was out and all the boys would come into town, because there was a Pima reservation nearby. We just forget that we are runaway boys. We bought some bread and crackers, and then I thought we should follow the Salt River. It was sure hot, and every once in a while we would go to the river and jump in it to get cooled off.

It was kind of late when we got up to the mountains where the

Salt River and the Verde River come together. When we got up there I said to Paul, "Where do you want to go?"

"I want to go home."

"All right. You can go on home. Just as soon as you get home they are just going to bring you right back."

"Where are you going?"

"I think I will go down to Florence, and I can catch a train then and cross the state line there in Las Cruces. Just as soon as I get across the state line I can look for a job. It doesn't make any difference what kind, just so I will have something to eat every day. If you want to go home, just go to it."

"But I can't go home alone."

"Why can't you? Here's the Salt River. If you follow this Salt River, you will come to a place where there is a Yavapai reservation. That is much closer than following this Verde River up."

"I don't know."

"Well then, Paul, if you want to go home, we will go together. So let's go."

We crossed the Salt River and went across the Verde River and went up to Fort McDowell. Just before we got there we ran into some Mexicans. It happened that I knew one of those Mexican boys. I had met him in Mesa City once when I was working there at the soda fountain for a while.

He said, "Eddie, what are you doing up here?"

"Oh, I'm just taking my vacation up here."

"Well, I am glad to see you. How about some watermelon before you go on?" He went to his watermelon patch and brought us a nice ripe melon. We cooled off. After we ate the watermelon and rested, we went on.

We went on until we came to a house that was up there. We were afraid to go near any house where there might be a white man, because you never can tell whether they might have gotten a message that two boys had run away. So we didn't go to the house, but as we were going by and we looked in through the door, we saw that it was a store.

As we were going on farther, somebody yelled. We looked up there and saw a Yavapai. He called us and waved his hand to us, so we went over. Just as soon as we got there we saw that he was an old man. He made an awful war whoop and yelled. Just as soon as he stopped, another fellow comes out of his place and yelled. Then all the rest of the people in the place did that. Then they all came up to the place where they first heard the man yell. That was the signal that someone has arrived.

None of them could talk English, and we ourselves could not understand them. One or two of them could understand a few words of English. They wanted to find out who we were and what tribe we belonged to. When they started naming all the different tribes, finally one said Moca. We knew before that the Hopi had been called Moqui.

After finding out who we were, then they began to talk among themselves and try to tell us what they were talking about. The nearest we can make out was that the Yavapai and the Moqui were pretty close friends. By this time there came around a boy they had sent for who could speak English. Finally he went all over what they had been telling us to be sure that we understand.

They told us that the Moqui was pretty hard to beat in times of war. They said that the Moqui uses the boomerang. They said that that was the thing they were afraid of. If the boomerang hits you, it will go right through you, where the arrow makes only a little hole. They were telling us that once they attacked the Hopi, and most of them were killed because of the boomerangs. They said that we were friends. We were sitting in a circle, and we were put in a place where the most respected person would sit.

After everything was over, all the older people smoked. They gave us a pretty good supper, and we slept there that night. The next day we thought we would just rest there because we don't want to be seen around and get caught and sent away from that place. We went into the willows growing along the river. We hid there in those willows all day. After it got dark we went back, and the next morning just as soon as we had something to eat we started out.

Before we started out they were trying to tell us where the trail was that leads over the mountains to Camp Verde. When we started off we tried to follow that trail, but we didn't go very far before we played out for being thirsty because it was so hot, so we headed back to the river. We thought we would never make it to the river, we were so dry. We came to somebody's old abandoned shack which had a well beside it. We ran to the well and looked down there and found an old dead coyote, so no chance to get water there. We went on again, and finally we got to the river all exhausted. We had a drink of water and laid down to rest. After we got cooled off, we drank some more. Then we went on.

We thought we would make a shortcut across the hills. We tried that, and as we were going along we found cactus of all kinds were ripe. Then again we got so thirsty and we thought that we would get some moisture out of something. We found some of these prickly pears, but we were so dry we couldn't swallow it and could barely even spit out the seeds. We had gone too far from the river, so we got on top of a hill to look for it. There it was about three hundred to five hundred feet below. We knew we had to get out of there and climb down to get any water, so we started down.

Paul was going ahead of me, a little further on. I wasn't trailing right behind him. About halfway down I ran on to a rattlesnake about four feet long and three inches in diameter. I was scared. I jumped over to one side and picked up a rock. He was just about ready to strike when I threw the rock and hit him right on the head. It killed him dead. I just looked at it for a while, and the rattle was going back and forth. Finally it quieted down. I jumped down and took out my knife and cut the rattles off, tied them up and put them around my head. Then every time I make a move I hear a rattlesnake.

When we got near the river there was at least ten or twelve feet of sheer wall. We looked around to find out how we are going to get down. Finally, we found where some of these wild grapes were growing, and the vines were hanging down. I reached down and grabbed a vine and slid down on it. These vines were about six or eight feet down, so I got near enough I just jumped the rest of the way down.

We were exhausted from thirst. Finally we got cooled off and came to again. We looked up and saw a lot of swallow nests in the holes in the wall. We started throwing rocks at them. We knocked down a few and then went on. We decided to stay with the river.

This was a little past noon. Before we left that morning the Yavapai had given us a roll of tortillas, and Paul was carrying it. So it was past noon, and I turned around and asked him if he still had the lunch.

"Yes."

I looked around and there was only two pieces of tortilla left. He had been eating it all the way! I sure bawled him out.

"Don't eat that anymore. You never can tell when we can get anything more to eat, because it seems like nobody is living in this part of the country." I thought that we were going to have those tortillas when we do get real hungry. "Better let me carry them. If I eat all of it, it would be all right, because you have had yours already." I was very much disgusted, and he wasn't keeping up with me. He was dragging along.

It was pretty close to sundown and we were still on the river, crossing it every once in a while. We hadn't seen anybody, either. We found a good soft spot on a bank and laid down. We were hungry, but we didn't dare to eat the tortilla. I used it for a pillow so it won't get away from me.

We were far down in the canyon. It was bright moonlight. We had
lit a little fire, and Paul soon went right to sleep. As I was laying
there I heard something. I raised up and saw a coyote coming by,
heading for the water. I was watching it. I thought I would scare the
coyote, so I felt around for a rock and threw it. The coyote got so
scared it ran off west on the hill and made a big war whoop. I got
right up and made my war whoop in answer.

Paul woke up. "What's the matter?"

"That was just what I expected," I said. "You have been having a
bad dream and you have been talking with that old coyote."

"I didn't say a word. I wasn't talking to anybody."

"You can't fool me."

"You mean to say I have been talking with that old coyote?"

"Sure."

"I was sound asleep."

"Don't let me catch you again." So then I laid down and went to
sleep. We were really tired. We slept until after sunrise, got up, and
washed our faces.

Then I said, "Come on, let's go. We got to keep going."

By that time I was noticing lots of rabbits and doves that I could
have shot if I had had my bow and arrows, that we could roast and
eat. It was almost noontime. "Paul, I will give you one tortilla, so if
you can eat half of it and save the other half for tonight, you will be
doing pretty well. I am not going to eat mine until I get real hungry. I
am still all right. Here's your share."

He took it and we went on. Afterwhile I looked back and he didn't
have any tortilla. "Paul, did you eat your tortilla already?"

"Yes."

"Don't ask me for any more. This is mine."

We didn't see a soul. The night came again, and I still had my
tortilla. We made camp again and the next morning got up and went
on. My tortilla was getting pretty hard and was dry and tough. Then

I got into the river and soaked the tortilla and wrapped it up in a handkerchief. I kept feeling to see if it was soft enough, and it was, so I ate it about noontime. We didn't see anybody at all that second day.

That night we had to make camp again. I said to Paul, "Tomorrow is our last day. We might go through the day, but I don't know about the next day. So, better brace up. I know you have been worrying, and that is the reason you have been dragging behind me. Just say to yourself that you are a man."

He didn't say anything.

We slept again on the riverbank. The next morning I said, "Now, Paul, remember what I said last night." Then we started out.

When we got hungry and tired, we took a big drink of water. It was about noontime and pretty hot when we came to a road which was more like a trail. Right on the riverbank a sign said, "Ranch 15 miles." I didn't know what "15 miles" meant because I didn't know anything about the long measure, so I thought that it might be just a short walk. We stood there for a while, looking at the sign. Then I said, "Why don't we walk to this ranch? We might find something to eat there. It's only fifteen miles."

"That's up to you."

"Let's go."

We started out. I don't know how far we walked on that road. It may have been a mile. Anyway, we couldn't go any farther. The same thing happened. We were exhausted with thirst and couldn't go anymore, so we turned back. We started toward where we thought the river was, and we walked and walked. Finally we came to a wash, kind of a deep ravine. I started down the steep bank, where water had been going over. I found some shade and sat down. Finally Paul came sliding down the hill. He sat down by me. I said, "Paul, I'm through. This is my last resting place. Now, if you had just been man enough like you always had acted at school! Think it over. Think over your smartness, how you always talked at school, bragging about yourself. If you are man enough, get on the other side of the bank from here, and we will watch each other to see who will die first. Don't look at me that way. I have already told you I am done."

"I think I will just stay here by you."

"All right."

I had been in the hot sun and now I was in the shadow. I sat there a while and got cooled off. I looked at Paul, and he was sound asleep. I got up and waked up Paul.

"Paul, there is no time to sleep. We aren't going to die here. Come on, let's go. If you are not all in, we will make it up on that bank."

We went down to the bottom of the wash and started up the other side. As I was going up I found a stick long enough to use for a cane and went on with it. We climbed out, and after a little ways came to another wash. When we got down in there we found holes. We just went searching around for water, and finally we found some water under a rock. We really went for it. I got the rock out of the way, and we got down and got a drink. But I couldn't hold this water; it all started coming up. After I got through drinking, I laid down and went to sleep. After I rested and cooled off, I went back to the water and looked down in there. It sure smelled and there was a lot of dead fish in it. I didn't get another drink.

"Let's go. This wash may lead to the river, because it has water in it." We must have come only about a hundred yards when we ran on to the river.

We decided not to leave the river again. I guess this was the third time we said we wouldn't leave the river. We crossed the river. On the other side I saw some mesquite trees just loaded with beans. I took a bunch of it and chewed on it, and it tasted pretty good. I knew that the Pimas would eat the mesquite beans. I got a handful and put some in my handkerchief. We ate quite a lot and felt very good.

Evening came again, and we didn't see anybody. There wasn't a soul in that country. We camped again. We had gone through the day and were still alive. I said to Paul, "We got through the day today, but I don't know about tomorrow. We can't go back. We just have to keep on going."

I took my map and looked at it. "We are closer to Camp Verde than we are to Fort McDowell. We will be lucky if we can reach Camp Verde. So we just have to go on." We slept down there somewhere again that night.

The next morning we got up. From having eaten the mesquite beans the day before, we felt pretty good. That stuff has good nourishment in it. It was about two o'clock in the afternoon and I was going ahead as usual when I saw a "bare" foot track. I stopped and looked at it. Paul was away behind me. When he finally came up I said, "Paul, you might just as well cry for your life, because there are bears in this valley. Here is a big bear track. If those bears happen to smell us, we are both dead."

He kind of hurried over and looked at it. "Do you call that a bear track?"

"Sure. From what stories I have heard, bears have feet like humans, so that must be a bear, because nobody human is here. Let's keep going."

"I wonder if we can't follow this track. Well, let's go on, we made up our mind not to leave the river."

We must have gone about fifty or a hundred yards when we came to another track. This time the track was made by a moccasin. "Well, somebody must be around here." Then we heard dogs barking a long way off. We went over the hill, and there was kind of a wide space with cottonwood trees growing in there. We saw the dogs running up toward us, and we heard somebody yell, so we kept on going up that way. When we got near to the cottonwood trees, we found somebody camping there, an old Yavapai woman.

Just as soon as we got to her, she got up and yelled a big war whoop. Somebody yelled back. The old lady motioned to us to sit down. She was looking at us, and soon two younger women came running in. Just as soon as they got there the old lady started rattling off, and I didn't know what she was saying. The two younger women got wood and started a fire. The older one started cutting up meat and began boiling it.

The old lady reached into a sack. We were so tired we didn't pay much attention to her, but after a while I noticed she was stirring something up in a basket. This basket was about a foot wide and eight inches high, and she was stirring something with her hands. Then she got up and brought it over to us with a cup, and she motioned for us to drink it. I took the cup and looked at it, and it was red, kind of cerise color. I took a cupful and tasted it, and it sure tasted good. I drank it and got another cupful and drank it down. I handed it to Paul. "It's all yours. You can drink all you want to. I am full." He drank the whole thing and put it down.

Now the meat was done. The old lady dished it out and put it in front of us and motioned to us to eat. We started eating, but before we got through we felt so sleepy that we quit eating and she cleared it away. There wasn't any bread. That was all that I had, just meat. We found out later that it was venison.

We kind of moved back and laid down, and I don't even remember going to sleep. Sometime way in the night I woke up and found that we had a cover on us, sleeping on the sand. The next morning I woke up way after sunrise. It was getting hot.

"Paul, you better wake up, because it is late. We can't sleep here all day. We have to go on." He got right up and rubbed his eyes, and I looked at him. He could hardly open his eyes. He had been so sound asleep that he had forgotten to cover his face, and the mosquitos were so bad they must have covered his face up.

Just then the dogs began to bark and kept running up the hill. Here comes two men, coming in with game on their backs. They had two more deer. Just as soon as they got there—there was already a big fire and a lot of live coals—they took one of the ribs and roasted it on the live coals, and that was our breakfast. Then we asked them how far is it to Camp Verde. One said, "Two days' walk and one night's sleep. You take this meat." They gave us one side of the ribs for our lunch. They told us that they were going in to Camp Verde that day because their food supply was gone. They didn't have any flour.

We went on. We didn't want to leave the river, so we just followed it. That noon we had the roasted ribs. After eating our roasted meat, we went on. Later in the afternoon somebody yelled and we looked up on the hillside. Those Yavapai were way up on the trail, but we were on the river. We kept going and didn't see anybody else all day.

Just about sundown it looked like we were going into a narrow canyon, and we heard somebody yelling and swimming in the river. I asked Paul to go up and see who it was. "I think you better go up and find out who it is. It might be some Indians or some white people."

That fellow wouldn't go up there. He was so timid and backward, and you just couldn't make him do anything. I told him, "If I go up there and find out who it is, if they take to me and be kind to me, I am not going to come back and get you. You can stay here."

When I got there it was some cowpunchers. They were two men and a woman and a boy about seven or eight years old. They were white. There was a big pool of water there, and they were teaching their horses to swim. They would get into this pool with their horses and make them swim out. That's what they were yelling about.

I got there, and it was just about suppertime. They asked me where I came from, and I said I came out of the water. Just about that time Paul came dragging up. "Where did he come from?"

"Oh, he came out of the water too."

"Two fish who just came out of the water? Is that your partner?"

"Yes, but he's all played out," I said. "How far is it to Camp Verde?"

"There is a trail here. This is as far as you can go, following the river. You can't pass through here, the canyon is too narrow. Where did you come from?"

"We came up from Fort McDowell, following the river. We have been on a trail for several days, and we found out we didn't have enough to eat or drink. If you can spare any food, I would like to have some and will be willing to pay you for it."

"Don't mention it. We'll give you something to eat." They told us they would help us out, providing we would kill a snake for them the next day. "You kill that snake and take his rattles if you want to. You can do that in the morning. The snake lives right over here at the foot of these rocks. He will come right out of that hole there, and every time we come near that snake it runs for its hole."

"We will get him tomorrow."

That night we slept in a pile of hay. They spread a canvas over it. Having a good supper, we slept good that night. The next morning, just as soon as we got up, we went out on a hunt for that snake. Sure enough, we found that snake there and he ran for the hole. It was kind of a crack in the rocks. We beat him to the hole and killed him and put it on a stick and took it over to the camp. They said, "That's the fellow." The man threw it in the fire and burned it up.

Before we left they put up some lunch for us—some peanuts and boiled potatoes and some jerky meat. From there we started climbing. There was a crack in the mountain, a kind of narrow canyon going right straight up the mountain. It was a sort of volcanic crack just about in the center of the canyon. We saw where those Yavapai had camped. It was quite a long ways up there through that narrow canyon—about four or five miles. It may have been less, but it sure seemed as though it was that far. We got on top and looked around, and I says, "Paul, there are the San Francisco Peaks. We are getting close to home! You better brace up now, because one of these days we are going to get home."

We started down. When we reached the bottom we found the Yavapai eating their lunch. It was noontime. We didn't want to stop, so went right on. From there on we were in a narrow canyon. As we were going along I found a cowbell and picked it up. It had a strap on it, so I put it around my waist.

There were pockets along the canyon. We got to one of those pockets and we scared out a gray fox. That place was so narrow, and that fox tried to get by us, but he couldn't because of the brush coming in from each side of the wall. We had fun with that old fox. Finally we got tired out and the fox got away.

We went on, and as we were going along we saw a big bird, and it looked brown. "Paul, there is a bird up there. I think it is a buzzard because it is too brown. It can't be an eagle because it is too brown for an eagle." I never had seen an old eagle, but I had seen young eagles on the Hopi housetops. We went up there, and it flew away. It was a buzzard sure enough, because it didn't have any white tail feathers. It went around the hill.

Then we heard a young eagle scream. I looked up and saw the nest way up on the side of the wall. There was kind of a slope down, and it was right up about ten feet above the slope. We started to climb up. We got halfway up the slope and out flew the little eagle. It didn't fly very far but kind of dropped down. We started to climb down, and just as soon as we got down to the bottom we took our shoes off and jumped in the river. We wanted to see who could get the eagle. I must have come about ten feet out of the river, and the sand was so hot I just couldn't get to the eagle. I went back and jumped into the river and got cooled off and ran out again. Paul did the same thing.

This time I got the eagle. Just as soon as I grabbed the eagle, the eagle grabbed me, too. That eagle didn't let me go. Every time I tried to put my fingers on its claws, they would go deeper. I looked around and saw a stick lying on the ground. I picked up the stick and hit the eagle on the head, and he went down. I took the eagle across the river. We sat there and waited for the eagle to come to, but he never came back to life again. "Well, it's dead. Anyway, we are going to take the feathers home. I get the eagle's tail feathers. It's my eagle. I am going to take the tail feathers and all the white feathers that I can make pahos out of. You can have the wing feathers."

We started pulling off all the feathers. We were feeling pretty good now, because we have something to eat and the Yavapais were nearby. When anyone goes on a trip, they always bring back a souvenir with them, and that is what we were doing. We got to have one; otherwise we won't be admitted in to the tribe. I took my school shirt off and tore it into strips. I wrapped the feathers with it until the bundle was about one foot in diameter.

I says, "Well, let's go on." It was getting late. Just below Camp Verde the canyon was very deep and very zigzag. So we had to go over the hill and down again. One place ahead of us we saw something going along the path. It was some turtles. There was a chance to get ourselves some turtles. We took our shoes off and laid down everything there and ran for them, but before we got there they jumped into the water. We went into the water, too, but they were too fast for us. We went back and got our things and went on.

We went up the hill, and there was a line of rocks up there. We looked around, and down on the other side there was a cliff there. It was a limestone wall, and there were many rooms where the water had been cutting away. I looked into one but couldn't see very far because they were so dark. I lit a match. Just as soon as I lit that match, the bats came out at me. We went along to every door, lighting a match just to see the bats act like that.

We looked down over the hill and could see smoke below. We crossed the river just as soon as we could. We came to a camp, and a man got up and yelled. Then all the men around there began to yell, just as the Yavapai had done before. After the rest found that we were there, they started coming in again. We had a big council that night, and finally this cowpuncher that we had met down below on the river came over.

"Let those boys alone. They belong to us. They must come to our camp."

"All right."

"They came to us way down the river. We will take them to our camp."

We went with them and stayed in their camp that night. We had some venison to eat. The next day we thought we would rest there for a day. We had our shoes pretty well worn out. We asked them if there was any store there, and they said yes. So we walked up there about half a mile and bought ourselves a pair of shoes. We bought ourselves everything, including another canteen, because we are going to leave the river. Here we asked about the roads and the trails.

The next day we started out. We wanted to come up on the old road. It seemed as though those hills were quite near, but it took us all day to get to the foot of them, to the northeast.

It rained all day, and we got soaking wet and cold. At the foot of the hill I saw a dog.

"Paul, there is a dog here looks like a deer or antelope. We must catch this fellow for lunch."

We trailed the dog all around. We didn't catch the dog, but finally we came to an old cabin. There was an old hog in there, in the middle of the floor. We went in and kicked the old hog out and built a fire. There was no fireplace, but it was cold and we had to have a fire. It was pretty smoky, but we spent the night there.

The next morning just before we got to the top of the Mogollon Rim, we met a man coming down. We asked him where Flagstaff was. It was a Mexican. Anyway, he understood "Flagstaff," but we couldn't make out what he was saying to us. Neither one of us understood any Spanish. But he had a couple of bottles. One was water and one was wine. He offered us a drink out of his wine bottle, but we were afraid because we don't want to get crazy. We had been hearing in those days that if you drink that stuff, you just go crazy. We didn't want to go crazy; we wanted to go home. We got up on top and had a drink of the water that we had gotten the day before, and we found some natural water tanks.

We were in the pine trees and it was getting late. We didn't know just where we were. As we were coming along we saw some houses and tents. It was cold to us, having come right out of Phoenix. We looked at one house and the door was open. We had an idea that some prospector must be living there. We went inside and found one old man there.

"Hello, mister." No answer.

I tried again, "Hello, mister." He didn't seem to hear me.

"Come here." I went over to him and put my hands to his ear. He said, "You got to yell as loud as you can for me to hear."

"CAN YOU GIVE US SOMETHING TO EAT?"

"Oh, you boys hungry?"

"YES, WE SURE ARE!"

"You boys go outside and chop wood and bring it in and start the fire."

We started the fire, and the old man got up from his chair and made some biscuits. I had some meat, so he cooked that, and we had some coffee. So we ate. Just a little while after we got through, two men came running in on horseback. One of these fellows went running up to the old man.

"Anything left that we can feed on? What became of that beef we killed the other day?"

"The rest of the party got it."

"Let's sweep their tents for any food they might have left. We have kind of been depending on you for all this time." Pretty soon they came back with a sack of canned stuff. It was tough in those days. I guess cowpunchers didn't give a damn what they did. They asked us to eat with them, and we did.

I kept looking at one of these fellows. I said, "Isn't your name Rex?"

"Yes."

"Do you remember little Eddie?"

"Yes."

"Do you know when I used to work at the big dairy, herding calves?"

"Yes. What are you doing up here?"

"I ran away from school."

"Good for you. Can you ride a horse?"

"Sure."

We spent the night there. The next morning the men said to take anything we wanted in the house for lunch. They made us a lot of biscuits and put them in a box, and we asked them how far it was to Flagstaff.

"Twelve miles. Just about take you all day."

I don't know how far we went from there. Then we thought the matter over. What to do? Suppose we got into the town of Flagstaff and find a policeman or someone waiting for us. They will get us right there and take us back to school before we get home. We turned off the road and headed east. We didn't know where we were going, except we knew we were going east. I thought that if we could get to the end of the ridge, we might look out and be able to look into the Hopi country. We couldn't see anything because the forest was so thick. We didn't see anybody, and when it got dark we were still somewhere in the cedars and juniper trees. It was so cold we started a fire. We thought we would dig a trench and if we ever reached a dry spot, we could sleep. We dug and dug until finally we got discouraged and tired, toward morning, and went to sleep.

Just before sunrise I woke up and heard a rooster crowing. I looked around. We must have been about three hundred yards from a house. It was a nice house, and we went over there, and sure enough we found two men. When we got there one says, "Hello, boys. Are you lost?"

"We don't know where we are."

"Where are you going? Where do you live?"

"Out here on the Hopi reservation."

"There is a canyon over here. If you go into that canyon, you will come right out under the railroad track. Come on in and have some breakfast, and then you can go on."

The breakfast was about ready. The food smelled so good—bacon and fried eggs and coffee. We ate a good breakfast. "Now you boys can get on to that canyon and be on your way."

We went into the canyon. This must have been Walnut Canyon. We followed the canyon for a ways, and then we heard the train whistle and climbed out and hurried toward where we had heard the whistle. Finally we came to the railroad. This must have been on the other side of Winona because it wasn't very long before we came out at Angel Station. As we were passing by we saw a lot of train cars, and we saw a woman through the window, cooking. By that time we were hungry again, but we went on. Then as we were going along there, way in the afternoon, the road crew caught up with us with one of those handcars. They picked us up and carried us a ways. Then we walked on. This must have been the place on the other side of Heber, on this side of Canyon Diablo. We could see the Canyon Diablo station. It looked as though it was just a mile away.

We hadn't got there, and the sun went down. When we got to the Canyon Diablo bridge, it was the most dangerous thing that we had done. Suppose we got caught in the middle of the bridge and a train came along? We got across, though, and went to the store. We bought some crackers and a can of peaches and canned meat of some kind. Might have been corned beef. We asked the man if we could have a place to sleep. He said, "I got two bunks over there, and you can go and spend the night there.

We went over there and knocked on the door. A man opened up and looked at us. "What are you two doing here?"

"We are going to sleep here tonight."

"The hell you are. You aren't coming in here."

"The hell we aren't. We are coming in just the same."

"I am going to beat you fellows up."

One of the fellows was just lying on the bed and didn't say anything. We went back to the store and told the man that they wouldn't let us in. He told us he would go over there. When he got over there he said, "These fellows are going to stay here tonight. You fellows sleep in one bed, and these fellows will use this bed. Do you understand?"

"Yes, yes, yes."

"Make some coffee," the owner said.

Then they were kind to us. We got our supper and went right to bed.

The next morning I woke up and I raised my head and said, "Start the fire. Get the breakfast. We want to eat."

"All right, all right, we catchem."[41]

41. This was probably Edmund's first contact with the many Chinese men working on the railroad in northern Arizona at that time.

11

The Scholar Returns Home

We had our breakfast, and we went to the store and got some crackers, because they didn't keep any bread. We filled up our canteen and went on. It was a long trip from there, and it was very hot. It was that year that the drought was so bad. We crossed the dry river and started in the direction of the Red Lake post office and store. I knew where it was because I had been there before. Just about sundown we walked into the store.

"Hey, you fellows don't look like Winslow or Flagstaff boys. You fellows been drinking?"

"No drinking. The river is dry."

He looked at me. "You fellows can't stay here. I can't trust you fellows."

"All right. You don't have to trust us. We can go on, but we want to buy something first."

"What are you going to buy?"

"We want to buy something to eat."

He reached down and took out a cupful of flour and said, "You boys don't need to buy anything here." He put the flour in a bag and pulled out a coffeepot and two cups and spoons and one cupful of sugar. "Now, you boys take this stuff over there to those Navajos and ask them to make you some bread and coffee. You're Hopi, aren't you? You don't look like Navajos."

We went over to the Navajos who were to get our supper. We didn't understand a word of Navajo, but they did make our bread and coffee, and we had our supper and spent the night with them. The next day we went back to the store. We took the coffeepot and all those things back. We asked him if we could have some more. "Yes, yes. You boys better have some more bread made, so you can have some lunch along the way." We wanted to buy some crackers. "I am not letting you buy anything. You ask them to make you some more bread." We took the stuff back, and they made some more bread for us.

After we had our breakfast we filled our canteens. It was another hot day. We used up all the water before we had gone very far, because it was so hot, and we knew that we had to find more. We were near the Polacca Wash. When we got to the wash there were signs that there had been water in the wash recently. We looked around and found some. It was thick and bitter, but we had to drink it. There wasn't enough to fill our canteens.

While we were resting near a big cornfield below Coyote Springs, we saw some men riding by on horseback. We didn't want to show ourselves, but after they all went on we followed them. My, it was a long walk. If we only had had nerve enough to show ourselves to those men, we could have ridden home on horseback.

We got up to the Burro Springs about sundown and decided to wash our faces. We washed our faces and filled our canteens and started out again on the road. It was getting dark. Just before we got to the hills, Paul played out. He called me back. "Well, I am getting cramps now. I am all in."

"Paul, we are not going to stop here. We have to make it up to the mesa tonight. You better lay down and let me work you over." He laid down and I started hitting him on the legs and muscles. "Now get up and see if you can go any better."

We didn't know how late it was, but we wanted to get up into the village. At that time there wasn't anything but a burro trail. We crawled up on to the bench, where the road comes up on the mesa on the west side of Mishongnovi. We started for Shipaulovi. Finally we got on top. We stopped in the plaza. I said to Paul, "I will go and see where my parents are."

I went up to the place where I last saw my parents, over the alleyway, but nobody was there. I jumped over to the clan house, thinking that they might be moved back into that house. But no. I went to the east corner of the plaza. I asked them there where my parents were. No one recognized me; I had to tell them who I was. They told me that my parents had moved into a relative's house, which had originally been our house. I went over there and found them. They were surprised to see me. I called Paul. The next morning Paul went home to Walpi.

Just about that time they were working on a new school plant at Keams, so I went to look for a job there. I worked around this new plant for two weeks and then went back home. It was Snake Dance time, and I wanted to go and see the dance, which was at Oraibi.

On the morning of the dance I went out early, before sunrise, to get one of my father's horses. I found the horse all right, but I couldn't catch him. There weren't any corrals anywhere near, and I chased after that horse all day with no luck. Then after sundown I started home. I did not have a darn thing to eat that day. I got home way after dark.

As soon as I got my supper I took my bedding and started off the mesa. I went down about halfway off the mesa and laid down there and was soon sound asleep. Somebody threw my covers off. I jumped up and somebody said, "I am looking for you."

"What do you want with me?"

"Don't ask me any questions. Just come along!"

"Come along where? I am going to sleep." I lay back down on my bed. This time he ran to me and just jerked me out of bed. Then he got me mad, so I went for him and grabbed both his arms. Then all at once he got hold of my hair and twisted my head. Then I reached out for his hair. I got ahold of him on the side of his head, and I just gave him a quick jerk and pulled him down. By this time I was wide awake, and I found out that he was a Hopi policeman.

He thought then that I was getting the best of him, so he pulled out his gun. I grabbed the gun, and I was lucky getting it away from him. I threw it away into the bushes. Then we started wrestling. He tore my shirt right straight down the front. Then I wanted to do the same thing, so I pulled out his shirttail and pulled his shirt right off his back. By this time he was ready to quit. So then he began to talk sense. He said that he did not mean to do any fighting. Then I asked him what he really wanted. He said, "The agent wants to see you in Keams Canyon."

I asked him, "How will I get there?"

"You have to walk."

"If I have to walk, I am not going. If the agent wants to see me, he can come out and see me at home. I have been out all day, and I am not able to go anywhere tonight."

He asked me again if I really meant what I said.

"Yes, you can't make me go anywhere tonight."

He said, "You have to go, because the agent has sent me here for you."

I told him that it didn't make any difference who sent him after me.

"Would you go if you could ride this mule? I would be willing to let you ride, if you would go."

"All right, I'll take the mule."

So I went on up home, and when I got into the plaza there was the mule. I went into the house and put on another shirt. I was ready to go. Just then two more policemen came. They were Navajo. Not noticing them, I mounted the mule and went off down the trail as fast as the mule could go. Then the two Navajo chased after me. It was so dark that those two poor policemen had a hard time to keep me in sight.

I got off the mesa way ahead of them. To do their duty, the policemen had to catch up with me. They caught up with me when we were three-fourths of the way to Polacca. We stopped about half a mile on the west side of the present-day school. These policemen said that we would have to wait there for two other Hopi policemen who were Walpi men. I took the saddle off the mule and tied the mule to a post. I laid down to sleep, using the saddle as a pillow. I was so tired I went right to sleep.

Then someone was shaking me and asking me to wake up. He said that we were going on. I was tired. I told them there was another day coming. They insisted that we had to go on. So they took the saddle from under my head and saddled the mule. I was still wrapped up in my blanket. I just would not get up. They asked me to get on the mule, but I did not want to. I said I was going to sleep there till the next morning.

So then the Hopi policeman asked the Navajo policeman to let me ride with him. So the Navajo got on the back of the saddle, and I was going to ride in front so he could have his arms around me. One Hopi policeman picked me up and started to put me on the horse. As he got closer I kicked the horse right in the nose, and the horse swung around and threw the Navajo off. Then they all got so mad! The two Hopi policemen grabbed me. Just then one more rider arrived, which was the chief of police.

He asked the rest of them what they were doing. They told him that they were trying to put me on the horse. The chief of police asked why they wanted to do that, so the other fellow says that they wanted to go on into Keams Canyon. The chief said, "What are you going to do when you get there?"

"We thought that there were orders that we had to get there tonight sometime."

The chief of police said, "There is no such a thing. The only orders are that we are to get these boys there sometime. When we get there we won't know what we are going to do."

Then the policeman said, "This boy has been making us a lot of trouble."

The chief said, "So I heard. If you only treat him right, he won't make any more trouble. Just let him sleep. There will be another long day tomorrow." So then the policemen unsaddled the mule, and all the rest did the same with their horses, and we spent the rest of the night there.

During the time they were trying to put me on the horse, Paul had arrived. They had brought him down from the First Mesa. I did not say a word to him because I would rather he would sleep. Before sunrise I was up and had saddled up the mule while the policemen were still asleep. Just about as I was ready to go off, one of the policemen woke up and gave the alarm, so they all got right up and started saddling their horses. Some of them were only half awake. There were five of them—two Hopi and three Navajo policemen. I did not pay any attention to them. I just got on the mule and went on towards Keams. They chased after me from there on. Paul was riding on back with one of the policemen. They caught up with me when I was crossing the Polacca Wash. I was just spurring the old mule. I didn't care, because it wasn't mine.

We got to Keams Canyon about eight o'clock. When we got there we went to the dining room to get our breakfast. We found out that we had to stay there and wait for a man who had come from Phoenix to come and get us. He was still out by Oraibi someplace. We had a long day there waiting for him. The policemen, too, had a long day, because they were watching us all day long. That night they told us that we were to sleep in the dormitory. After we got in there the man in charge showed us what beds to take. Then after going out he locked the door on us. So I picked up the chair and ran to the door and gave it a good bang, and here he comes back again. He opened the door and asked me what I was doing and what I meant. I turned around and said, "That is what I would like to know. What do you mean by locking us in? If you are going to keep us locked in, you will have the floor to clean in the morning. If you do not want to do that, you had better leave the door unlocked. We have no intentions of running away. It is too far to the railroad."

He said, "All right, I will leave the door unlocked."

The next morning after breakfast all the policemen came after us and said that we were going up to the office to see the agent. When we got into the office, we found a man whom we knew, Mr. Duclos.[42]

Just then Paul's parents came walking in. We were all standing up against the wall. No one was seated. So when Paul's parents came in, each stood on each side of him. So then the agent, a Mr. Charles Burton,[43] turned around to me and said, "Edmund, you have to go back to school down in Phoenix."

I said, "Mr. Burton, I am not going back. At least I do not want to go back."

So he said, "You have to go back. That is all there is to it."

So I said, "Mr. Burton, you heard me before. I have already said that I do not want to go back."

Then he said, "If the only way we can get you back there is to put you in chains and throw you in the wagon, then we will do it."

"All right. You can send me down that way, and the very day that I am there I will leave that place."

---

42. August F. Duclos joined the Phoenix Indian School as head carpenter in 1902 and had been sent to Keams Canyon to help persuade Edmund and Paul to return to Phoenix. In 1904 he is listed as superintendent of industries at the Phoenix Indian School.

43. Beginning around July 1, 1899, Charles E. Burton was superintendent of the Keams Canyon School and, in effect, subagent for the Hopi reservation.

"When we get you down there, we will have to put you in the guardhouse and keep you there."

"All right. They won't keep me there forever, and the very day that they let me out I will leave the place. I don't have to stay there. In fact, I do not want to go back to that schoolhouse."

By this time Mr. Duclos spoke up. He turned around to Mr. Burton and said, "Now Mr. Burton, I did not come up to arrest these boys. I have orders from the superintendent not to treat these boys in such a way as you have suggested, because I know that we at the school were at fault. This boy had a good reason to run away from there, and I don't blame him. So I think it is best that you let me handle this."

Mr. Burton said, "The reason that I said all this is that it seems as though this boy is pretty hard to handle."

Mr. Duclos said, "Why, certainly he is now. Now, you must understand, dealing with the boys or children, you must treat them wisely, because the harder you go on any children, they will become hard to handle. As for my part, as long as I have been dealing with the boys in all the schools where I have been, I have treated them wisely and they always have made friends with me, and I have learned to like them. They are much more easy to handle that way than to be hard on them. So you let me take care of these boys like I want to."

Mr. B. said, "All right."

By this time I understand that Mr. Duclos had long been taking my side. He turned around to me and said, "Edmund, will you go back with me?"

I said, "Yes."

"When I do get you back there, you will be just like one of those newcomers. You are going to be treated right, and I will see that it will be done. Nobody will ever say anything to you. No one will ever punish you for what you have done. In fact, you haven't done anything, and I realize all the hardships that you have gone through to get up here. Everything will be all right."

"All right. I will go back with you, providing that you will look after your promise."

"Certainly I will, and everything will be all right." Then he turned around to Paul and said, "Paul, will you go back to Phoenix with me?"

Paul did not say a word. He could not, because he was crying. I was so mad I looked at him and started bawling him out in Hopi. "Paul, what are you crying about? Are you crying because you are still nursing? If you are, have some more before we go. I never did see such a baby as you are."

Finally he said that he will go back, but all this in a half-crying tone. All this time the interpreter had been telling the Navajos all that I had said, and that I had put up a great protest. So when everything was fixed up, we came out of the office. Just as soon as we had come out, all the policemen rushed up to me and wanted to shake hands with me because they had never seen anyone say such things to the face of the agent. They were all afraid of him. I did not want to shake hands with them, so I did not, not after the way they had treated me on the way in.

We were then ready to leave the Keams Canyon School for Phoenix. We found out that we were not going alone. There were some others going down with us. So that morning we started out in the covered wagon for the railroad at Holbrook. We were two days on the road to Holbrook. This time I knew better what to do on the train. We got to Phoenix in the night, and this time we went up on the streetcar, not on a hayrack. When we got there Paul and I went straight to our rooms and found our beds still there. At least I did. I don't know about Paul.

The next morning, just as soon as we heard the bugle we got up and washed ourselves up and waited for another bugle to blow to go to the line. When it did blow, we went out to the line, and the boys were rather surprised to see us, and everybody rushed up and was shaking hands with us. Then, after getting into line as usual, we were marched up to the dining room. When we got inside of the dining room, all the eyes were on us because they did not know how we had gotten back again. From there on we were just like the rest and waited for the school to be opened up again.

Oh yes, something important I forgot to mention. My grandfather had died about the first of the year in 1902. I got a letter about two weeks after his death, in January. That is why I did not expect to see my grandfather when I ran away from school.

While I was home, Father told me what Grandfather had said before his death. He did not have a chance to tell me everything. My grandfather had said that the time would come that everything would come to light that he had told me before he had sent me away. He asked my father to remind me of the things which he had taught me, that he was really sincere that I should carry on what he has wished me to do, as he really believed that the things which he had learned from his grandparents will surely come to pass someday.

So when I went back to school I knew that I would have to spend two more years there. I made up my mind to do the best I could. So during that time I really had to study hard, to show the teachers that I could really do better if I was treated right.

I picked up another Bible study and put two more years into it. When my time finally came to leave the school, I really was glad to go back home.

On June eighteenth I boarded the train for Winslow and got there the next morning. I did not know where to go. I had not sent any word home that I was coming. I guess it was because I was so anxious to leave school. I wondered how I was going to get out to the reservation. Then I met some friends whom I had worked for down in Phoenix. I accidentally ran into them in Winslow. They asked me to come up to their house and stay with them, and I did.

But I was anxious to get out home, so one morning, without saying a word to anyone, I started out northward, thinking by going that way that I might reach the Hopi towns. I went as far as the Little Colorado River, about twelve miles. I did not realize how far it was out to the reservation. I stopped with some Navajos there someplace. They tried to talk to me, but they could not make me understand. Nor could I make them understand anything that I was telling them. One of the Navajos must have thought that I wanted to go back to town. So he got his horse ready and we rode back into Winslow.

When I got there, I found my uncle Kachina had arrived from Phoenix. I asked him if he had sent word home, and he said yes. At the same time he was asking me if I had seen anyone coming in from the reservation in a wagon. I said no and that I had just got back in on horseback. Then I told him what I had done, that I had started out on foot but had to come back with the Navajo. So then he said we would have to wait until the wagon came so that we could go out home.

We waited about two days. Then the wagon came. It was his brother-in-law who came with the wagon. The next day we loaded up our trunks into the wagon and started homeward. It was a long trip by way of Red Lake and up through the Polacca Wash. We were about four days on the road. We got home about the twenty-eighth of June, 1904.

12

The Boy Becomes a Man

So I was home again from school. Just like any young fellow, I had big ideas of doing things on my own, not anything I had learned in school. But I had taught myself to weave a blanket Hopi-style down in Phoenix. Finding that my father had a lot of yarn that was prepared, I thought I would try it out.

A few days later the missionary came up and asked me to go to church the next Sunday. I knew that my mother had been going to the church all the time I was away, so I told the missionary that I would be glad to come any time that I had the chance. She said that I would have a chance on Sunday. That is the day that the people go to church.

When Sunday came around, my mother went down, but I did not go. When she returned that afternoon, she started asking me questions about what she had heard in the lesson. I explained a few things to her, but not being educated she could not very well understand.

She asked me, "Do the dead really go to heaven?"

I said, "Mother, I have never yet seen anyone going to heaven."

Then she said, "The missionary has said that all the good people who go to church, when they die they will go to heaven. And the bad people will go down into the underworld and have their punishment on the way down. And when they get there they will be put into the firepit—like a pit where we bake corn—by the devil."

Then I said to Mother, "Well, I don't doubt the missionary is telling you all this. What I really think is that she just wants to keep you scared so that you will come to church every Sunday."

She did not ask me any more. The only thing she said was that I might have learned something about all these things, because Grandfather has sent me to school to learn the truth. I told her that I will tell her the truth. I told her that I wanted to find out first what she learned at the mission.

So that Sunday went by, and the next, and I did not go to church. Mother did not go that time, either. Then the next Sunday came around. This was about the fourth Sunday. Since my mother did not go to church, someone had told the missionary that I was against the church. Monday morning when I was working hard at my loom, on a blanket, I heard someone call in English from the ladder, "Edmund."

I turned around and there was the missionary. I said, "Yes? Would you mind coming in?"

She said, "No. But I would like to see you in So-and-So's house. I am having a meeting there."

"All right, I'll be coming around right soon."

So then I got up and came down off the ladder and went around to that other house. When I got there the house was full of people, men and women. There was not much of a space for me to sit down, so I just sat down beside the door where I went in.

I could see the fire in the missionary's eye, and all of a sudden she said, "Edmund, would you be man enough to stand up and then talk to me? I hear that you have been saying a lot of things about me and my church, so I want to see if you are man enough to stand up and talk to me and answer my questions."

I just sat there and stared at her. I was mad, so without getting up

I said, "Miss McLean,[44] would you be lady enough to step forward and make me get up? Then I will talk to you. If not, I'll just sit right here."

So then she said, "Edmund, I did not think that you would be this vulgar."

"Miss McLean, did you say vulgar?"

"Certainly I did."

"Miss McLean, you must have been hearing things in your sleep."

"Nothing of the kind. The people that come to my church have been telling me that what I teach down there is contrary to your belief."

"It might be because of what I have seen and heard around here. The only thing you have done for these people whom you have supposedly converted is to take them out of one superstition and get them into another."

"What I teach is not superstition. This is a real good religion."

"It would be if you would only preach the gospel and practice what you preach. You have been telling these people that if they miss one Sunday and do not come to church, that they are condemned. Now is that not superstition? What I learned was that God never condemns nobody. Any person that doesn't go to church, that tries to do something, to do a little work for themselves, or to go and see the dance somewhere, you tell them that they are condemned and you just throw them out of the church."

She burst into tears and ran out of the house. As soon as she got out she got on her horse and started for home. I got up and went home. I did not even try to explain what had happened. I just left the people wondering.

From then on, this missionary and I were pretty good enemies. Wherever we happened to meet, she would not even look at me. So I never had gone to the church till the new party had taken the place

---

44. Miss Mary McLean was a Baptist missionary at Second Mesa at this time.

over. As soon as any of these missionaries insisted on my going over there every Sunday I just quit, because if I wanted to read the Bible I just stayed at home.

At the same time, I was listening and looking around very carefully, because I wanted to study my own people's side. From then on I was in all the ceremonies and had been initiated into most of them, because I was following what my grandfather had asked me to do. For, as he said, it was the only way to find the truth.

When I was off the reservation, I never refused any booklets of any kind or from any denomination, because as I knew, some of these churches were publishing such booklets on the way they believe in their religion. I found out that all these religious denominations differ but that they were all heading for one point. I do believe that no one really knows what is going to happen hereafter, but this has never been brought out in any publication of any one church or denomination.

My grandfather had said, "What has been told to the ancestors many years ago will surely come to pass." I feel that we are in that stage today, with all this world's distress. Grandfather had said that we would be in the midst of this trouble, that the end will come when every soul is drunk by fear. I believe that something is going to happen. The world will come to an end. And on that day the wicked will be done away with as my grandfather had stated. Whoever will do away with the wicked will not be the Bahana that we are seeing today. I do believe now that he whom the Hopi call Bahana is the heavenly God.

By the time I came home, Father had begun to believe in God. He also practiced as a medicine man. When Father was called upon to work on a patient, he would hold up his right hand as you do when swearing in court and look over his right shoulder. Pretty soon the hand would begin to tremble as if he were experiencing an electric shock, and then he would rub his hands together and work on the patient.

To the people he appeared to be a very peculiar fellow. Although he was considered to be a medicine man, he would hardly ever give any medicine. He would just work over a person. Most troubles would be like constipation. Those people blamed such ailments on worries that they had. After my father worked over a patient like that, he would say, "You are all right. There is nothing wrong with you. You are just worrying." Then he would tell the people that if they would only try not to think about what people are saying about them or what had happened, they would forget their worries and be all right. The people expected that he would tell them that some person, some witch, was causing such calamities. But he never would tell anybody that. He would just tell them to get up and go their ways and they would be all right.

People would wonder at his holding his right hand up and his looking over his shoulder and looking into the heavens. One time his nephew Roscoe asked him about that, why he always did that before putting his hands on a patient. He looked at Roscoe and laughed. He said, "I have found that a good many people come to me pretending to be sick. If a person is just pretending, or if they really do not want to get well, I do not receive any power from God. But if an honest person comes and wants to get well, it does not take long for me to feel the power coming through my hands."

Then Roscoe asked him if there is such a thing as a heavenly God.

"Certainly. If there were not, we wouldn't see the wonders of life and death, and the changes from season to season."

Roscoe said, "Why do these people that teach us the Bible—or these missionaries—hate to work on Sunday?"

Father told him, "They are just hypocrites. There is no such thing as Sunday. Sunday is just like any other day that we are put here on earth to do whatever our hands can find to do."

Father had visions from God. He said that every human being and every creeping thing on the face of the earth had their time to live and their duty to perform. He said that whatever moves, it moves by

God. He told Roscoe, "So whatever you do, always remember what I have been telling you. Because I myself see now that my father, who is your grandfather, really did know and has told us the truth. All the Hopi ceremonies are wrong. So you do not have to be initiated into the *wuwutcim* ceremony if you do not want to, because you will only waste your time there." So Roscoe never has been initiated into any ceremony. He is the only Hopi of his age today who is free from all ceremonies.

After that summer that I had trouble with the missionaries, I went into Keams Canyon to look for a job. When I got there the superintendent was very nice to me. It was the same guy that had wanted to send me down to Phoenix in chains. He said it would be all right if I came in and just did odd jobs around the school. I went back home for a few days and then went over there.

I was there about two months when the chief from Shipaulovi sent for me, saying that there was something very important that he wanted to talk to me about. So I went out, and when I got there he was already waiting for me. I asked him what was so important.

He said, "I think it is time that I should look into this matter of the land that was promised to my ancestors when they founded Shipaulovi. I feel that this land now rightly belongs to me and to my people here at Shipaulovi. I want to see how Shungopovi feels about this theory. In order to get these things right, I would like to have it written down. So as I tell it to you, I want you to write everything down."

I asked him why he should want to do this. According to his theory, he should take over all of the land which had belonged to Shungopovi. I thought that, being a chief, he should know what he was talking about. I got my tablet and pencil and wrote everything down as he told it to me day after day.

But I only got his side of the theory and nothing from the Shungopovi chief. I began to feel that he was only going to scare up trouble. Once or twice he called for the agent, and he would come out and we would talk about the matter in the kiva. I would let the agent read the papers that I had written down. Of course I knew that the agent did not agree with him, but at the same time the old chief wanted the Washington authority to back him up. This is the reason that he wanted me to write everything down so those papers could be shown to the Agency.

As we were going strong against Shungopovi for its land, it happened that one morning as I was out after my horses and driving them in, I ran across some of the horses that belonged to the old chief. As I was driving them up to the mesa on one of those narrow trails around the ledge, it happened that a woman was coming down the trail. The first horse that came up saw this woman and got frightened and jumped back, knocking one of the other horses over the ledge.

That horse fell about fifteen feet. He tried to get up but fell back again. I made the old horse get up. She fell back again, and this time I could not get her up. I left the horse there and reported to the old chief. He demanded that I pay for the horse. He said that it would cost me ten dollars. He wanted cash, and I told him I had no money. He said that he might have to take one of my horses. I told him that my horses were worth more than ten dollars. So then he decided to call the police to act as authority and judge.

That evening a policeman came up, and I told him that the best thing that I could do would be to give the chief a buckskin and two dollars, which I thought might cover the damages. The policeman went to the chief. When he came back he said that the chief would not take what I had offered him. I told the policeman that I was through.

A few minutes after the policeman had left, the chief came around to the house and said that I ought to have money. I told him that because of him I had left my job in Keams Canyon, and if he did not appreciate what I had been doing for him he could get out of the house. I was through. He was rather surprised, because no one had ever said anything like that to his face. He said I must be a witch like my grandfather. I said that he must be a witch himself. I told him that all that I had learned about his theory, that everything would be exposed, that the people of Shungopovi would hear all the secrets of what he was planning to do against them. Of course he did not realize that I would tell them such things. At last I told him that he would never be able to get his hands on Shungopovi land and that I was through with him and would never interpret for him again, not even one word to any white man. I was so darn mad that I did not know what to do.

The next morning I saddled up my horse and bid my parents goodbye and said that I might not be back for a few days. That day I left the Hopi towns and went out to the Navajo country. I did not know a word of Navajo. It seemed as though the whole world was dark around me then.

I got to the Navajo country that evening. I got off my horse and went into a hogan and sat around with the Navajos till the sun went down and it was dark. Then I unsaddled my horse and hobbled it and turned it out to graze. The next morning I showed no intentions of leaving. The Navajos must have wondered why I did not go away. It was customary as long as I stayed there that I would have to be fed.[45] After a few days I made up my mind that I should be doing something for my grub, and I tried to make the Navajo understand that I could herd sheep for them. I finally did, and from then on I had some sheep to herd. I went out every day with the sheep.

One day they got a Navajo that could talk English, and they got him to ask me why I was staying there with them. I told them that I would like to stay with them and herd sheep because I did not have a job anywhere and that I did not have anything to do at home. So

45. Even though in 1882 the federal government had officially approved partitioning the Navajo and Hopi reservations, the astonishing episode Edmund reports here is an example of turn-of-the-century intertribal acceptance and friendship.

then the family thought that it was all right for me to stay here and help them herd sheep.

All this time the chief had been sending out his nephews, and they had been all over the country looking for me. They did not know where I was. In fact, I did not want them to know. I had been home more than once, but it was always at night. I would leave the horse down below and just walk up. If I wanted anything in the way of provisions or corn or piki, my father would help me carry it down to the horse. Afterward I heard a lot of talk that someone had seen me here or there, and things like that. One fellow, who was supposed to be my uncle, thought that he was pretty smart and told the chief that he would go out and look for me, and if he ever found me, he would bring me in dead or alive.

I happened to be up that night, and my parents had heard about it, so then I wanted to find out if my uncle really would be man enough to do it. So that night, instead of going to the Navajo country, I went down to Burro Springs to look for my other horses. Somebody had caught sight of me that night and knew that I had been home. So early in the morning they traced me down to Burro Springs. I rounded up my horses at Burro Springs good and early and got on the best horse and went off.

As I was going over the hill that runs along the north side of Polacca Wash, I looked back and saw my uncle coming down from the north side toward Burro Springs. He asked the sheepherder there if he had seen me. He told him that I had just left a little while ago. So this uncle started out after me. He met a couple of his friends on the way, and from there on they chased after me.

Just before I got to the Jeddito Wash, I looked back and saw two riders followed by a third coming after me. These two fellows came up on each side of me and stopped right in front of my horse.

"Where are you going?"

"I am going home."

"Then you are going in the wrong direction. You must be crazy."

I already knew what had been said about bringing me in dead or alive. He had gotten hold of the reins of my bridle, and I knew that I could not do very much. Anyway, I moved up close and reached for his reins. I was mad and so was he. He was asking me why I was going out to Navajo country, and I told him that was none of his business. That made him worse. I did not want to tell him anything.

All of a sudden I just put my spurs into my horse's ribs. He jumped and I just turned my uncle's horse clear over. He had a quirt, the loop over his wrist. I had his reins and a loop of this quirt around my saddle horn, and I just jerked him right out of his saddle. He got up on his feet and hung on to my reins. He got up close and said, "My dear nephew, I did not intend to get you mad."

I said, "I know that you have good intentions, sure. I have already heard that you will bring me back home dead or alive."

"That doesn't mean anything. In fact, I did not really mean what I said."

I said, "Why act it, then, like you did? I do not care what you do. I know that none of your people like what I have said to your chief. If you are really going to stand up for your chief, do your stuff and act like a man. I know anybody can talk like a man, but they cannot always do what they say."

Then he came to his senses and he begged me to return. We turned around and started back toward Burro Springs. We argued all the way down to Coyote Springs. Most of the argument was on the clan house and that I should go back to the clan house and take up the fraternity chieftainship and try to do all I could for the benefit of my people. I told him that I never would do that. He asked me why several times, but of course I did not want to expose myself yet, nor my grandfather's theory.

Everything was brought up in those questions concerning the Hopi ceremonies and also the missionaries, that I might have some intentions of getting baptized and just desert my authority as being a chief of the One Horned Fraternity. I told him that I was not telling him anything very much concerning myself or what I was going to do in the future. The only thing I said to him was that he would just have to watch and see what I would do. I said that if he didn't like what I did, he didn't have to like it. I told him to take possession of the clan house and give himself the authority to be the chief of the One Horned Fraternity, and that I was through with that fraternity.

The sun went down and it was getting dark. I left those three guys there and went over to the sheep camp at Coyote Springs. The next morning I went on back to the Navajo country. Within a year's time I was talking pretty good Navajo, and the family that I was living with, they got so that they thought a lot of me because I did look after the horses and cattle and sheep, and they could always depend upon me. So then the Navajo, they gave me about twenty-five head of sheep within a year's time, and the man gave me two horses.

This old Navajo thought that I really would stick if I got married over there. So there was a Navajo woman who had been to school, and they thought I might marry her. About shearing time they made good money, and this old man gave me thirty dollars and said that I could go to this woman and give her the thirty dollars and then everything would be all right and I could then live there. But just as soon as I got the thirty dollars I went after my horses and beat it for home! I did not go back for two months.

When I did return to Navajo country, I asked the old man for my sheep. His wife, whom I called Mother, acted mad. She pretended she was awful mad. Anyway, instead of giving me twenty-five sheep, they gave me five more, extra, and asked me to come back in the fall and they would give me a steer that I could butcher. When fall came around, I went over there with a wagon and butchered the steer. From then on I would visit the family once in a while. My Navajo mother died about three years ago.

One day I was chasing my horses because I wanted to go to the Snake Dance. I was hungry and thirsty and I saw smoke over in the distance, near the Polacca Wash, south of Shungopovi. I went that way, thinking that I might get something to eat or at least a drink of water. When I got there I found that there were several people gathering green sweet corn. The smoke that I had been watching during the day was coming out of a firepit in which these Shungopovi people were going to bake sweet corn. They gave me water out of a pottery jug. It was nice and cool and I felt very much refreshed.

The last load of sweet corn was coming in sacks on a burro. These were added to the sacks of corn around the edge of the firepit. The pit was dug about six feet down into the adobe clay. It was about five feet in diameter at the bottom and got narrower toward the top. When I got there I looked into the firepit. The hole was red hot; you could hardly come near it. The man who was putting the fuel in had to stand about five or six feet away from it when he threw in the wood.

Everyone took their places around the pile of corn. The man who owned the corn pit had corn of four different colors, representing the four directions, wrapped up inside of some snakebrush. Pulling it away from each direction in turn, he threw it down the mouth of the firepit. Quickly we all pushed the rest of the corn into the pit with our feet. At the same time we selected a few good-looking ears for ourselves. While we were doing this, the owner was busy filling the ventilator—a shaft at one side about as deep as the pit—with a bunch of cornstalks and a lot of dry dirt. When all the corn was set into the pit, it was full clear to the mouth. The owner rolled a large, flat, round flagstone over the opening, which was only about two and a half feet wide. Cornstalks and leaves were put over that, and then a lot of dry dirt to seal it.

Then someone started a bonfire nearby, where we roasted the ears of sweet corn we had saved. Most of these people were from Shungopovi, and I did not know who they were. I later learned to know all of them, after I was married. Several girls were there too. But, being a stranger, I was a little shy, and I did not even talk to the girls at first. It is customary that a Hopi boy should not make friends with a girl the first time he meets her; it would be kind of awkward for both of them.

While we were there roasting our corn, though, I did meet one of them. I decided that I was not going to be shy any longer. When evening came, we ate and talked together. Within a year, one of those girls and I were married. You might say that that evening my childhood was over.

Reference Materials

Bibliography

Bartlett, Katharine

1934   Spanish contacts with the Hopi, 1540–1823. *Museum Notes* [Museum of Northern Arizona, Flagstaff] 6 (12): 55–60.

1981   Alfred F. Whiting, 1912–1978. *Journal of Ethnobiology* 1 (1): 1–5.

Beaglehole, Ernest, and Pearl Beaglehole

1935   *Hopi of Second Mesa.* American Anthropological Association, Menasha, Wisconsin.

Boslough, John

1990   The enigma of time. *National Geographic* 177 (3): 108–132.

Bradfield, Richard Maitland

1971   *The changing pattern of Hopi agriculture.* Royal Anthropological Institute of Great Britain and Ireland, London.

1973   *A natural history of associations: A study in the meaning of community.* 2 vols. Duckworth, London.

Brumble, H. David, III

1981   *An annotated bibliography of American Indian and Eskimo autobiographies.* University of Nebraska Press, Lincoln.

1988   *American Indian Autobiography.* University of California Press, Berkeley.

Burton, Charles E.

1902   Report of the school superintendent in charge of Moqui. Submitted 7 August 1902 to the U.S. Commissioner of Indian Affairs, Washington, D.C.

Carroll, John B. (ed.)

1956   *Language, thought, and reality: Selected writings of Benjamin Lee Whorf.* MIT Press.

Clifford, James

1988   *The predicament of culture: Twentieth-century ethnography, literature, and art.* Harvard University Press, Cambridge, Mass.

Colton, Harold S.

1969   Edmund Nequatewa, 1880(?)–1969. *Plateau* [Museum of Northern Arizona, Flagstaff] 41 (4): 154–155.

Cory, Kate T.

1907   Hopi diary. Manuscript no. 208-2, Library of the Museum of Northern Arizona, Flagstaff.

Courlander, Harold

1970   *People of the short blue corn.* Harcourt Brace Jovanovich, New York.

1971   *The fourth world of the Hopis.* Crown Publishers, New York.

Cox, Bruce A.

1970   What is Hopi gossip about? Information management and Hopi factions. *Man* 5 (1): 88–98.

Curtis, Edward S.

1909   Indians of the stone houses. *Scribner's Magazine* 45 (2): 161–175.

1922   *The North American Indian.* Vol. 12: *The Hopi.* Plimpton Press, Norwood, Mass.

Curtiss, William E.

1905   Education and morals among the Navajos and Pueblos. *American Antiquarian and Oriental Journal* 27: 259–264.

Dennis, Wayne

1940   *The Hopi Child.* Appleton-Century Company, New York.

Diehl, H. C.

1955–   H. C. Diehl Hopi archives. Compiled by P. David Seaman.
1975   Approximately 7,000 manuscript pages, 8,000 Hopi vocabulary cards, and 14 tape recordings. Manuscript no. 226, Library of the Museum of Northern Arizona, Flagstaff.

Dockstader, Frederick J.

1954   *The Kachina and the white man: A study of the influences of white culture on the Hopi Kachina cult.* Cranbrook Institute of Science, Bloomfield Hills, Mich.

Donaldson, Thomas
1893 *Moqui Pueblo Indians of Arizona and Pueblo Indians of New Mexico: Extra census bulletin.* U.S. Census Printing Office, 1893.
Dorsey, George A., and Henry R. Voth
1901 *The Oraibi Soyal ceremony.* Field Columbian Museum, Chicago.
1902 *The Mishongnovi ceremonies of the Snake and Antelope fraternities.* Field Columbian Museum, Chicago.
Dunaway, David K., and Willa K. Baum (eds.)
1984 *Oral history: An interdisciplinary anthology.* American Association for State and Local History, Nashville, Tenn.
Eggan, Fred R.
1950 *Social organization of the western pueblos.* University of Chicago Press, Chicago.
Fewkes, J. Walter
1892 The ceremonial circuit among the village Indians of northeastern Arizona. *Journal of American Folklore* 5 (16): 33–42.
1903 *Hopi Katcinas: Drawn by native artists.* Twenty-first annual report of the Bureau of American Ethnology to the Secretary of the Smithsonian Institution, 1899–1900. U.S. Government Printing Office, Washington, D.C.
1907 Hopi. In *Handbook of American Indians north of Mexico,* edited by Frederick Webb Hodge, 560–568. Smithsonian Institution, Bureau of American Ethnology, Bulletin 30. U.S. Government Printing Office, Washington, D.C.
1927 The Katcina altars in Hopi worship. In *Annual Report of the Board of Regents of the Smithsonian Institution for the Year Ending June 30, 1926,* 469–486. U.S. Government Printing Office, Washington, D.C.
Forde, C. Daryll
1931 Hopi agriculture and land ownership. *Journal of the Royal Anthropological Institute* 61: 357–405.
Fraser, James H.
1969 Indian mission printing in Arizona: An historical sketch and bibliography. *Journal of Arizona History* 10 (2): 67–102.
Greene, Helen-Margaret
1955– Helen M. Greene Indian archives. Unpublished notes, 5
1985 binders, compiled by P. David Seaman. Library of the Museum of Northern Arizona, Flagstaff.

Hall, Sharlot M.
1907   The Indians of Arizona. *Out West* 27: 471–497.
Hieb, Louis A.
1979   Hopi world view. In *Handbook of North American Indians,* vol. 9:
        The Southwest, edited by Alfonso Ortiz, 577–580. U.S. Govern-
        ment Printing Office, Washington, D.C.
1991   Review of *Religion and Hopi life in the twentieth century,* by John D.
        Loftin. *American Indian Culture and Research Journal* 15: 147–149.
Hinton, Richard J.
1878   *Hand-Book to Arizona: Its resources, history, towns, mines, ruins,
        and scenery.* Payot, Upham and Company, San Francisco.
Hodge, Carleton T.
1968   Indian summer. *Language Sciences* 3:2.
1969   Hopi field materials. Unpublished fieldwork materials, includ-
        ing 20 tape recordings, 50 sound spectrograms, and 1,000 vo-
        cabulary cards, included in the P. David Seaman Hopi Archives.
        Special Collections and Archives Department, Cline Library,
        Northern Arizona University, Flagstaff.
Hodge, Frederick Webb (ed.)
1907–   *Handbook of American Indians north of Mexico.* 2 vols. Smithso-
1910   nian Institution, Bureau of American Ethnology, Bulletin 30.
        U.S. Government Printing Office, Washington, D.C.
James, George Wharton
1908   *What the white race may learn from the Indian.* Forbes, Chicago.
Kennard, Edward A., and Edwin Earle
1938   *Hopi Kachinas.* J. J. Augustin, New York.
Klein, Barry T. (ed.)
1992   *Reference encyclopedia of the American Indian.* 6th ed. Todd
        Publications, West Nyack, N.Y.
Kluckhohn, Clyde
1945   The personal document in anthropological science. In *The use
        of personal documents in history, anthropology and sociology,*
        edited by Louis Gottschalk, Clyde Kluckhohn, and Robert An-
        gell, 79–173. Social Science Research Council, New York.
Laird, W. David
1977   *Hopi bibliography: Comprehensive and annotated.* University of
        Arizona Press, Tucson. The definitive Hopi bibliography
        through 1975.

Loftin, John D.

1983   Emergence and ecology: A religio-ecological interpretation of the Hopi way. Ph.D. thesis, Duke University. University Microfilms International, Ann Arbor.

1991   *Religion and Hopi life in the twentieth century.* Indiana University Press, Bloomington.

Lowie, Robert H.

1929   Notes on Hopi clans. American Museum of Natural History, *Anthropological Papers,* 30: 303–360.

McCluskey, Stephen

1980   Evangelists, educators, ethnographers, and the establishment of the Hopi reservation. *Journal of Arizona History* 21: 363–390.

Malotki, Ekkehart

1983   *Hopi time.* Mouton Publishers, The Hague.

Marriott, Alice

1945   *The ten grandmothers.* University of Oklahoma Press, Norman.

Miller, Wick R.

1984   The classification of the Uto-Aztecan languages based on lexical evidence. *International Journal of American Linguistics* 50: 1–24.

Mindeleff, Victor

1891   A study of Pueblo architecture: Tusayan and Cibola. *Eighth Annual Report of the Bureau of American Ethnology to the Secretary of the Smithsonian Institution, 1886–'87.* U.S. Government Printing Office, Washington, D.C.

Mooney, James

1901   Dr. Joshua Miller. *American Anthropologist,* new ser., 3: 592.

Mottor, Carol Nepton

1991   Hopi healing practices. M.A. thesis, Department of Anthropology, Northern Arizona University, Flagstaff.

Murdock, George P.

1972   Hopi. In *Ethnographic bibliography of North America,* compiled by George P. Murdock, 3d ed., 215–322. Human Relations Area Files, New Haven, Conn.

Nagata, Shuichi

1970   *Modern transformations of Moenkopi Pueblo.* University of Illinois Press, Urbana.

Nequatewa, Edmund

1936   *Truth of a Hopi, and other clan stories of Shungopovi.* Edited by
        Mary-Russell Farrell Colton. Library of the Museum of North-
        ern Arizona, Bulletin 8. Flagstaff.

1942   Why the Spaniards called the Hopi "Moqui." *Plateau* [Museum
        of Northern Arizona, Flagstaff] 14 (3): 47–52.

1946   The place of corn and feathers in Hopi ceremonies. *Plateau*
        [Museum of Northern Arizona, Flagstaff] 19 (1): 15–16.

Nequatewa, Edmund, and Alfred F. Whiting

1957   Three Hopi texts. Manuscripts no. 140-2-1 and 140-2-2, Mu-
        seum of Northern Arizona, Flagstaff.

O'Kane, Walter C.

1953   *The Hopis: Portrait of a desert people.* University of Oklahoma
        Press, Norman.

Ortiz, Alfonso (ed.)

1979   *Handbook of North American Indians.* Vol. 9: *The Southwest.* U.S.
        Government Printing Office, Washington, D.C.

Page, Jake, and Suzanne Page

1982   *Hopi.* Harry N. Abrams, New York.

Page, James K., Jr.

1975   A rare glimpse into the evolving way of the Hopi. *Smithsonian* 6
        (8): 90–101.

Parsons, Elsie Clews

1939   *Pueblo Indian religion.* University of Chicago Press, Chicago.

Philp, Kenneth

1973   Review of *The Hopi Indians of Old Oraibi: Change and continuity,*
        by Mischa Titiev. *Arizona and the West* 15: 191–192.

Prucha, Francis P.

1976   *American Indian policy in crisis: Christian reformers and the
        Indian, 1865–1900.* University of Oklahoma Press, Norman.

Qoyawayma, Polingaysi

1964   *No turning back: A true account of a Hopi girl's struggle to bridge
        the gap between the world of her people and the world of the white
        man.* Edited by Vada F. Carlson. University of New Mexico
        Press, Albuquerque.

Sarris, Greg

1990   Review of *American Indian autobiography,* by H. David Brumble
        III. *American Indian Culture and Research Journal* 14: 130–133.

Schmedding, Joseph

1955   Christmas in Keams Canyon. *Desert Magazine* 18 (12): 8.

Seaman, P. David

1974–   P. David Seaman Hopi Archives. Approximately 50,000 pages of
1992   ethnographic data from original fieldwork as well as from numerous other sources. Includes approximately 40 tape recordings, 100 sound spectrograms, and 30,000 vocabulary slips.
Special Collections and Archives Department, Cline Library,
Northern Arizona University, Flagstaff.

1977   Hopi linguistics: An annotated bibliography. *Anthropological
Linguistics* 19: 78–97.

1985   *Hopi dictionary: Hopi-English, English-Hopi, grammatical appen-
dix.* Northern Arizona University, Anthropological Paper No. 2.
Flagstaff.

Sekaquaptewa, Helen

1969   *Me and mine: The life story of Helen Sekaquaptewa.* Edited by
Louise Udall. University of Arizona Press, Tucson.

Sexton, James D. (ed.)

1981   *Son of Tecun Uman: A Maya Indian tells his life story.* University
of Arizona Press, Tucson.

Spicer, Edward H.

1962   *Cycles of conquest: The impact of Spain, Mexico, and the United
States on the Indians of the Southwest.* University of Arizona
Press, Tucson.

Stephen, Alexander M.

1936   *Hopi journal.* Edited by Elsie Clews Parsons. 2 vols. Columbia
University Contributions to Anthropology 23. Columbia University Press, New York.

Talayesva, Don C.

1942   *Sun chief: The autobiography of a Hopi Indian.* Edited by Leo W.
Simmons. Rev. ed. Yale University Press, New Haven.

Titiev, Mischa

1937   The use of kinship terms in Hopi ritual. *Museum Notes* [Mu-
seum of Northern Arizona, Flagstaff] 10 (3): 9–11.

1944   *Old Oraibi: A study of the Hopi Indians of Third Mesa.* Peabody
Museum of American Archaeology and Ethnology, Harvard
University, Cambridge, Mass.

1972   *The Hopi Indians of Old Oraibi: Change and continuity.* University of Michigan Press, Ann Arbor.

Trennert, Robert A., Jr.

1975   *Alternative to extinction: Federal Indian policy and the beginnings of the reservation system.* Temple University Press, Philadelphia.

1988   *The Phoenix Indian School: Forced assimilation in Arizona, 1891–1935.* University of Oklahoma Press, Norman.

Turner, Christy G., II, and Nancy T. Morris

1970   A massacre at Hopi. *American Antiquity* 35: 320–331.

United States. Commissioner of Indian Affairs

1895–   *Annual Reports.* House Executive Documents. U.S. Government

1904   Printing Office, Washington, D.C.

United States. Department of the Interior

1899   *Statistics of Indian tribes, Indian agencies, and Indian schools of every character.* U.S. Government Printing Office, Washington, D.C.

Vandever, C. E.

1890   Report of Moqui Pueblo Indians, Navajo Agency. *Annual Report of the Commissioner of Indian Affairs to the Secretary of the Interior* 59:167–172. U.S. Government Printing Office, Washington, D.C.

Voegelin, C. F.

1941   North American Indian languages still spoken and their genetic relationships. In *Language, culture, and personality,* edited by Leslie Spier, A. Irving Hallowell, and Stanley S. Newman, 15–20. American Anthropological Association, Menasha, Wis.

Voegelin, C. F., and F. M. Voegelin

1957   *Hopi Domains: A lexical approach to the problem of selection.* Supplement to *International Journal of American Linguistics* 23 (2).

1977   *Classification and index of the world's languages.* Elsevier Publishers, New York.

1985   Archives of the languages of the world. Archives of Traditional Music, Indiana University, Bloomington. Includes extensive field data on Hopi language and culture collected by the Voegelins and other researchers.

Voth, Henry R.

1905   *The traditions of the Hopi.* Field Columbian Museum, Chicago.

Wallis, Wilson D.
1936   Folk tales from Shumopovi, Second Mesa. *Journal of American Folklore* 49 (nos. 191–192): 1–68.
Wallis, Wilson D., and Mischa Titiev
1944   Hopi notes from Chimopovy. *Arts and Letters Papers* [Michigan Academy of Science] 30:523–556.
Waters, Frank
1963   *Book of the Hopi.* Viking Press, New York.
1969   *Pumpkin Seed Point.* Sage Books, Chicago.
Weber, Steven A., and P. David Seaman (eds.)
1985   *Havasupai habitat: A. F. Whiting's ethnography of a traditional Indian culture.* University of Arizona Press, Tucson.
Whiteley, Peter M.
1985   Unpacking Hopi "clans": Another vintage model out of Africa? *Journal of Anthropological Research* 41:359–374.
1986   Unpacking Hopi "clans" II: Further questions about Hopi descent groups. *Journal of Anthropological Research* 42:69–79.
1988   *Bacavi: Journey to Reed Springs.* Northland Press, Flagstaff.
Whiting, Alfred F.
1936   Hopi Indian agriculture: I, Background. *Museum Notes* [Museum of Northern Arizona, Flagstaff] 8 (10): 51–53.
1937   Hopi Indian agriculture: II, Seed source and distribution. *Museum Notes* [Museum of Northern Arizona, Flagstaff] 10 (5): 13–16.
1938–   A. F. Whiting Hopi notes and papers. P. David Seaman, compiler and editor. More than 21,000 pages of Whiting's study and field notes relating to the Hopi compiled into 81 topical binders. An index volume and a user's guide are being prepared. For further information, contact Dr. P. David Seaman, Department of Anthropology, Northern Arizona University, or the Special Collections and Archives Department, Cline Library, Northern Arizona University, Flagstaff.
1978
1939   *Ethnobotany of the Hopi.* Museum of Northern Arizona, Bulletin 15. Flagstaff.
1962   To see ourselves: Word from an anthropologist. *Practical Anthropology* 9 (May–June): 138–141.
1963   God and man. *Aegis* yearbook, page 28. Dartmouth College, Hanover, N.H.

1964   Hopi kachinas. *Plateau* [Museum of Northern Arizona, Flagstaff] 37 (1): 1–7.
1965a   Hopi nocturne. *Plateau* [Museum of Northern Arizona, Flagstaff] 37 (3): 99–105.
1965b   The bride wore white. *Plateau* [Museum of Northern Arizona, Flagstaff] 37 (4): 128–140.
1971   Leaves from a Hopi doctor's casebook. New York Academy of Medicine *Bulletin* 47 (2): 125–146.

Whorf, Benjamin Lee
1946   The Hopi language, Toreva dialect. In *Linguistic structures of Native America*, edited by Harry Hoijer et al., 158–183. Viking Fund Publications, New York.
1950   An American Indian model of the universe. *International Journal of American Linguistics* 16: 67–72.

Winship, George Parker
1896   *The Coronado expedition, 1540–1542*. Bureau of American Ethnology, Annual Report 14. U.S. Government Printing Office, Washington, D.C.

Wissler, Clark
1917   *The American Indian: An introduction to the anthropology of the New World*. Douglas C. McMurtrie, New York.

Wood, John J., Walter M. Vannette, and Michael J. Andrews
1982   *Sheep is life*. Northern Arizona University, Anthropological Paper No. 1. Flagstaff.

Wright, Barton
1973   *Kachinas: A Hopi artist's documentary*. Northland Press, Flagstaff.
1975   The legend of the Hopi Kachina. *Phoenix Magazine* 10 (12): 40–43, 66.

Index

ABOUT THE EDITOR

P. David Seaman, an anthropological linguist, has long been interested in American Indian studies. He was collaborating on the revision of Alfred F. Whiting's *Ethnobotany of the Hopi* at the time of Whiting's death in 1978. Since then he has worked on compiling and editing Whiting's extensive ethnographic notes and papers, and with graduate student Steve Weber, he edited *Havasupai Habitat: A. F. Whiting's Ethnography of a Traditional Indian Culture,* published by the University of Arizona Press in 1985. Seaman's *Hopi Dictionary* also appeared in 1985. He holds a Ph.D. in linguistics from Indiana University, has taught in Canada and Greece, and joined the Department of Anthropology at Northern Arizona University in 1967.